FOIE GRAS, MAGRET, AND OTHER GOOD FOOD FROM GASCONY

FOIE GRAS, MAGRET, AND OTHER GOOD FOOD FROM GASCONY

André Daguin and Anne de Ravel

Drawings by Karl W. Stuecklen

Random House New York

Library of Congress Cataloging-in-Publication Data
Daguin, André.
Foie gras, magret, and other good food from Gascony.
Includes index.
I. Cookery, French—Gascony style. 2. Gascony (France)—Social life and customs. I. Ravel, Anne de.
II. Title.
TX719.2.G37D34   1988   641.5944'77   88-42669
ISBN 0-394-67027-8

Manufactured in the United States of America
2 3 4 5 6 7 8 9
First Edition

Typography and binding design by J. K. Lambert

To Ariane Daugin

Acknowledgments

Most of all I am grateful to Melanie Menagh for her thorough research and editing.

My sincere thanks to all my Gascon friends, especially Maurice Coscuella and Roger Dufourt for being so generous with their cooking and their great stories of the region. Also to Dominique Sans, a patient guide.

And finally, many thanks to Pierre Franey, for his friendship, for lending me his kitchen to test the recipes of this book and for sharing his invaluable expertise.

ANNE DE RAVEL

Contents

Introduction

*S*everal years ago French cuisine experienced one of its periodic U-turns. The highly refined sauces and dainty presentation of nouvelle cuisine seemed to lack spontaneity; many felt it was too precious, too contrived, and too distant from the regional cooking traditions that, after all, had made up the fondest culinary experiences of most chefs and cooks. A wave of culinary nostalgia started to gain momentum; people began returning to their roots, digging into their heritage. The result is that regional cuisines have been rediscovered, the so-called *cuisine bourgeoise.* Since then, good cooks every-where have been conjuring up simple, delicious food, robust stews, heady cassoulets, and lusty soups—the kind of fare typically found at a neighbor-hood bistro behind steamy windows, served by congenial, overworked wait-ers in white aprons, accompanied by hearty wine and heated conversation. These earthy recipes share the same appeal of strong flavors and soul-warm-ing effects.

These are the essential elements of the cuisine of Gascony, a remote, hilly region in southwestern France, in the shadow of the Pyrenees between the Atlantic and the Mediterranean. The region's peasant cuisine has not changed significantly over the centuries. The farmers of the Gers region of Gascony eat the same food that their grandfathers' grandfathers ate and enjoy it just as much for its compelling simplicity and heartiness. The flavors of Gascon cuisine are strong and robust. The dishes are typically pungent with the essenses of mushrooms, game, duck, foie gras, cloves, and garlic.

Gascony is characterized by a tranquil, dreamlike landscape. The hills are topped with medieval fortresses, the hillsides and valleys dotted with sheep and rows of golden sunflowers. It is an area that tends to be less traveled (and hence less spoiled) than others in the south of France because it is relatively inaccessible, lying, as it does, south of the main road linking Toulouse and Bordeaux.

When Gascon cooking is discussed among Frenchmen, the name of André Daguin most assuredly arises. From the most dazzling French celebrities to the most humble devotees of the pleasures of the table, they make their pilgrimages to the Hôtel de France, expressly to experience the exquisite mysteries of Gascon cookery as practiced by its premier proponent.

My own passion for Gascon cuisine began long before I had the pleasure of dining with Daguin. It was nurtured at the home of my grandparents, who settled in the northwest of Gascony in an area known as the Landes. Each

of my visits was an initiation into the local cuisine. *Garbure* and duck-flavored lentil soups were often served. On special occasions my grandmother would open a jar of duck or goose *confit* purchased from a local farm. She knew which farm women produced the best foie gras and *confits,* two of the region's richer delights.

The recipes, of course, were a great secret, passed down only through the family from mother to daughter. The woman who made the best *confit* or foie gras inevitably became renowned for miles around, for such achievements did not go unnoticed. When my grandmother moved away from the Landes, she tried to obtain the secrets to carry with her; the women all just laughed and gave the same response: "I will send my *confits* and foie gras to you wherever you are, but I will not part with my recipes." And so, every year my grandmother ordered her supply.

The making of *confit* remained a mystery to me until I moved to Toulouse and asked one of my aunts, Chatoune, if she could teach me this mysterious art. Each November, Chatoune and her friend Annie would travel to a local market to buy fatted ducks to prepare their winter supply of *confit* and foie gras. They got together and cooked furiously for three days so that their preserves would be ready for Christmas.

I wasn't really much help—I just cut up the meat and tried to stay out of the way as the two women bustled about the tiny kitchen permeated with the scent of garlic, thyme, and *quatre épices.* Each knew exactly what to do, each had her station. Chatoune and Annie gossiped as they put the meat in herbs and salt to marinate. Handling the delicate foie gras with great care, they soaked it in milk and salt, then cooked it right in the terrine. This scene might have occurred in any Gascon kitchen, in the tradition of a cuisine perpetuated by the women of the house—*la cuisine des femmes.*

In his own kitchen André Daguin earned his reputation by creating his improvisations on these traditional Gascon themes. Over the years I had heard about Daguin from friends who insisted that there was a fantastic chef in Auch, that I must make a point of going there. One year, I finally made arrangements to see for myself.

My father and I set out from Béziers (about two-hundred miles to the southeast of Auch) at nine o'clock one warm, sun-drenched autumn morning. It was a three-hour drive. We left the highway at Toulouse and drove the last hour along a narrow, winding road through lush fields, past rambling houses, ancient villages, tiny farms, and small châteaux. Finally we spied the belltowers of Auch sitting high on a hilltop. We drove up Auch's steep streets as the drab, modern buildings of the new town gave way to pretty, old houses, finally arriving at Place de la Libération.

The entrance to the Hôtel de France is on a corner of the square. It opens into a pleasant lobby with a staircase leading up to the rooms and another leading to the bar/bistro. To the right, an imposing glass door swings open soundlessly onto a grand dining room—the size of a ballroom. The space is lit by a row of tall windows along one side, which add warmth to the ochre walls, the rust-colored, cloverleaf banquettes in the center of the room, and the giant sprays of flowers.

The restaurant was nearly full that day, yet tranquil and civilized. The room was hushed—*feutre*—like the inside of a felt box, filtered by the drapes and carpeting. We sat in the center on one of the banquettes—deep and plush, allowing one to survey the room and catch snatches of conversation, mostly heated discussions of local politics.

André Daguin, a strapping, handsome man with an expansive smile, came out to greet us. He gave us his menus, but volunteered to produce a special tasting meal for us. The result was a five-course feast of game, truffles, and assorted foie gras. The foie gras was served twice, first cold and then hot—and oh, what servings. They comprised a lesson on the cuisine of Gascony, hinting at the infinite pleasures of foie gras. The plate of cold terrines consisted of a foie gras with Sauternes, foie gras cured then frozen "in a towel," another flavored with tomatoes, and finally one cured in salt.

We were instructed to taste them in order, from the most delicate to the strongest. I was surprised and excited by this array of choices. It was like entering a whole new world of taste—before this I had only been exposed to traditional *terrine de foie gras,* seasoned with salt and pepper. All of these new preparations were like discovering that one could wear shoes of any color with a ballgown.

We continued our meal with hot foie gras *en papillote* with langoustines, which was presented on a little metal tray holding burning coals to keep it hot. The contrast of the briny fresh shellfish and silky foie gras made for a wonderfully complex combination of flavors and textures. We followed with squab, wild mushrooms, salad with truffles, and an assortment of desserts made with prunes. And, after such a regal Gascon repast, a glass of vintage Armagnac was a must.

A FEW WORDS ABOUT GASCONY
AND THE GASCONS

The enigma of Gascony and its people begins even when you try to pinpoint the region on a map. There is a broad range of opinion on precisely where Gascony begins and ends. I once asked André Daguin to define Gascony. "The borders of Gascony are elastic," he answered, after a moment of reflection. "The 'petite' Gascony includes the entire Gers *departement* and a small part of the *departements* surrounding it. The 'grande' Gascony is the entire southwestern corner of France." I was overwhelmed and confused by this statement, especially when he added with typical Gascon bravado, refer-

Auch

Auch's present tranquility belies a past of great energy and importance. Auch has always been considered the capital of Gascony. The earliest records of the city date back to 25 B.C. when the town was named Augusta, after the Roman Emperor Augustus. Augusta became an important Roman way station and market town between Toulouse and the sea.

Presently Auch, a town of twenty-five thousand five hundred Gascons, is the capital of the *département* Gers. From the pastures and cornfields, for miles around, the spires of the cathedral of Sainte Marie can be spotted, towering serenely above the Gers River, which flows through town and bisects the city into its old and new quarters. The cathedral provides a hub for the old city on the place de la Libération—the Hôtel de France is ensconced along one side.

Scrambling down the hill, from the spaciousness of the Place de la Libération, is a labyrinth of stepped lanes called *pousterles*, bordered by tall Gascon houses.

In the summer, next to the cathedral on the Rue Arnauld de Mole, you'll find a market, selling the fruits of the surrounding farms in pretty much the same way as has been the fashion since the eighteenth century: the market is crowded, aromatic, and full of all the noises necessary for commerce.

ring to the reign of Henri IV, "But then, of course, once upon a time, Paris was in Gascony. . . ."

For the purpose of this volume, we will define greater Gascony as the area from the south of the Garonne river to the Pyrenees. In the west, this area is known as the Landes, essentially a flat coastal plain consisting of vast woodlands and marshes. The soil can be so soggy that until recently many Landais performed their farm duties on stilts to prevent them from sinking into the mire. To the south and the east, lying between the forests of the Landes and the factories of Toulouse, the horizon becomes more varied as you enter the primary Armagnac-producing region with its ordered chains of vineyards coursing through the hills. Farther south, jutting into the foothills and then into the high country of the Pyrenees, is the Bearn, whose rugged country and independent philosophy have produced many equally rugged and independent Gascons, including Henri IV, who is still referred to with great affection as *notre Henri*.

While the area of Gascony may be difficult to define, there is nothing uncertain or ambiguous about the Gascon character. The people here claim that "every Gascon travels with a piece of clay stuck to his sole," alluding to the thick, heavy soil of the region, but also referring to the Gascon's unshakable pride in the good earth of his home.

Despite the territorial debates, this region holds itself distinctly apart from the rest of France. A true Gascon is before all a Gascon, cherishing his unique heritage and history with pride. When Charlemagne rode with his armies to attack Montauban, the Gascon scouts ran back to their fortress shouting, "The French are coming! The French are coming!"

Even the language is different. The elders speak a patois which has sadly become all but unintelligible to their grandchildren. Gascon, one of the tongues of southern France, is held by those who speak it to be more expressive and metaphorical—as though a Frenchman needs license for that. When Michel de Montaigne, a native Gascon speaker, was frustrated by the French language's inadequecy for giving vent to his emotions in his powerful philosophical treatises, he would cry, *"Que le Gascon y aille!"*—"You must use Gascon here!"

Another great writer was also sensitive to the dramatic proclivities of the Gascon people. In his *Travels in the South of France,* Stendahl wrote "Everything is done by fits and starts or on a sudden impulse. . . . In France, the South complains loudly because the North surpasses it in the arts of commerce. The answer is very simple: The south has natural genius, but the north has exceptional capacities and characteristics which would ensure success in business."

I am not sure that a Gascon would take umbrage at Stendahl's observation. More than likely, he would not be at all upset at being surpassed in the "arts of commerce." Gascony is a rural farming region whose population is less

than two thirds of what it was two centuries ago. There has been an exodus to Toulouse, Marseille, and Paris; and consequently the people who live in Gascony now are there because they choose to be, because they like their quiet, unhurried life of "natural genius."

Not that the living is necessarily easy—Gascony is a province that has always known the hardships of poverty. Indeed, after d'Artagnan arrived in Paris in the late 1630s, the tale of the impecunious younger son of Gascony saddling his horse and riding off to seek his fortune in the capital became a standing joke in Parisian theaters. But the Gascon warrior was also portrayed as a man of bravery and ingenuity.

Today's Gascons carry the legacy of ingenuity in their blood. Aside from this, one can't help but notice the spontaneous generosity, the happiness they derive from sharing their country, food, and wines. They have a genuine desire to make those they meet like Gascony and understand it. They enjoy being among friends, telling tall tales or laughing about themselves. The hunting season is an excuse for camaraderie. So are the numerous festivals around the region, such as the world championship for magret eating or the world championship of *pétanque*. It is not unusual to see young and old Gascons break into a traditional song while sharing a *pastis* at a café.

The nature of the Gascon is reflected in the region's cooking—earthy, individualistic, and spirited. With cooks on both sides of the Atlantic returning to the restorative pleasures of the home and hearth, the time has come to celebrate the pleasures of Gascon cuisine.

FOIE GRAS—BUYING AND HANDLING

$\mathscr{A}$nyone who journeys to southwest France in late fall to visit the colorful and cacophonous foie gras markets inevitably gets swept up by the soaring spirits of Gascons and their neighbors and by the excitement over their treasured foie gras, one of the world's most coveted delicacies. When it comes to celebrating the fruits of their labors, even the buoyant Bordelais have nothing over the rugged farmers of Gascony.

Foie gras (pronounced "fwah-grah"), literally "fat liver" in English, describes the oversized livers of fattened, specially bred geese or moulard ducks—*foie gras d'oie* and *foie gras de canard,* respectively. This increasingly coveted luxury food is produced in several regions of France, as well as in Hungary, a handful of other European countries, Israel and recently in the United States. Above all, though, it is associated with the province of Gascony. Other French producers are in Périgord, to the northeast, and Alsace, on the German border. To the people of Gascony, foie gras is much more than a prestigious agricultural product; it is also a cultural totem of sorts, an exalted symbol of a centuries-old tradition.

Foie gras markets in Gascony are open from late October through early April. Among the best known are those in the Gers towns of Seissan, Mirande, Gimont, Samatan, Fleurance, Eauze, and Riscle. Farmers stream into town from the surrounding countryside toting two-handled wicker baskets draped in white cloth containing the fresh beige livers of ducks and geese. It is the women, mostly, who are involved in the foie gras trade, for they are the traditional tenders of geese and ducks back on the farm. The production of foie gras is still, to a large extent, a cottage industry, with many small-scale producers supplying the markets.

The women's pride is palpable on market day mornings as they arrange their displays on long tables in rented stalls. This is an eagerly anticipated time of year, an occasion for isolated country people to mingle in the good natured—yet highly competitive—camaraderie of commerce.

The foie gras markets are decidedly democratic. No one except suppliers is allowed inside the market building until the shriek of a whistle at 10 A.M. signals the opening. Everyone—from retailers, restaurateurs, and commercial processors to housewives—has equal access to the sellers. At the appointed hour they circle the room, rubbing their chins, and inspecting the precious livers with the intensity of antique buyers, before loading up their baskets.

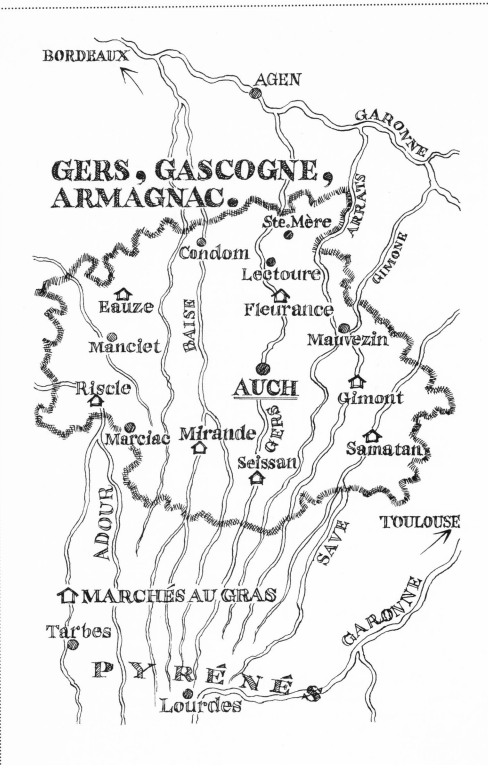

GERS, GASCOGNE, ARMAGNAC.

BORDEAUX

AGEN

GARONNE

ARRATS

GIMONE

Ste. Mère

Condom

Lectoure

Eauze

Fleurance

BAISE

Manciet

Mauvezin

Riscle

AUCH

Gimont

GERS

Marciac

Mirande

Seissan

Samatan

ADOUR

SAVE

TOULOUSE

GARONNE

⌂ MARCHÉS AU GRAS

Tarbes

PYRÉNÉS

Lourdes

By 11 A.M. most of the livers are gone. Another whistle pierces the room, inviting buyers into the duck and geese market. Freshly killed ducks and geese, minus their precious fattened livers, are laid out on counters, one after another, their necks dangling over the side. These birds are treasured for their flavor-saturated meat, much of which will find its way into *confit* that will be stored for a midwinter treat.

The market winds down shortly after noon. For many, the rest of the day is devoted to serious socializing in local bars and restaurants.

HISTORY

The technique of producing foie gras may indeed go back as far as the ancient Egyptians. Relief paintings on tombs dating from the fourth and fifth Egyptian dynasties (2600 B.C.) depict farmers holding geese by the neck and feeding them packed balls of grain, presumably to fatten them quickly. This method, called *gavage*, is fundamentally unchanged today. The rich diet causes the livers to swell up to four to five times their normal size.

Some have speculated that foie gras, like so many important inventions and recipes, was discovered by accident. As the theory goes, a farmer in Egypt had a flock of geese, and for some reason, one bird developed a nearly insatiable appetite; when killed for its meat, the farmer discovered that the oversized goose had an enormous liver that was exceptionally delicate and delicious.

Ancient Roman poems and literature are replete with tales of sumptuous banquets that featured the fattened livers of geese. According to at least one source, it is a Roman who deserves credit for advancing the technique of producing foie gras. Consul Quintus Caecilius Metullus Pius Scipio, the father-in-law of Pompey, a Roman general and statesman (106–48 B.C.), fed his geese a diet of figs to give the livers and the meat extra sweetness. A by-product was an enlarged liver with an ineffably delicate flavor. A half century later another Roman, Marcus Gavius Apicius, applied the technique to ducks and pigs.

Following the Roman occupation of Gascony the local people continued to produce foie gras. By the fifteenth century they had established a thriving cottage industry, first with geese, later with ducks. It was not until 1747, however, that the first published recipe turned up for *pâté de foie gras* in a book called *Le Cuisinier Gascon*, published in Amsterdam. It called for slicing fresh foie gras, seasoning it with truffles, and baking it in pastry.

The endless gastronomic skirmish over which is better, foie gras from ducks or geese, continues to this day. Some contend that the liver of a fattened goose is finer in texture, firmer, and tastier. But the duck partisans counter with the same ammunition. Who is right? Of course, it comes down

Foie Gras

5

to personal tastes. Undoubtedly the feud will spread to the United States if someday fresh *foie d'oie* is produced here.

United States law prohibits the importation of fresh meat, so fresh foie gras of any kind from Europe is unknown in this country. Imported foie gras is available only in cans. Processed canned duck liver, if properly made with quality products, has great appeal—it is firm, buttery and smooth, with a lingering, complex flavor that comes from slight aging in the package. However, its uses are limited—it is usually served as a pâté or added to stuffings. Federal law left little hope that the more versatile and fragile fresh liver would be available. Indeed, Paula Wolfert, in her comprehensive book *The Cooking of South-West France* (Dial Press, 1983) prefaced her remarks about foie gras by saying, ". . . it is doubtful that you will ever cook a fresh foie gras."

Ironically, the year that book appeared a group of farmers, some of them trained in Israel, were establishing a high-technology duck breeding farm in upstate New York's Catskill Mountains. The farm, called Commonwealth Enterprises Products Corporation, employs artificial insemination to cross-breed two very different types of ducks—the cantankerous Pekin and the genteel Muscovy—to yield moulards. Only moulards have the genetic makeup to produce fattened livers that equal the size and quality of those bred in France. The moulards are raised for fourteen weeks, reaching fourteen to fifteen pounds, before they are killed for their pale beige-pink livers, which weigh between one and two pounds.

This first domestic foie gras—at least on a large commercial scale—is now accepted enthusiastically by most French and American chefs in this country, many of whom maintain that there is virtually no detectable difference between the homegrown and the French-raised.

The growing availability of fresh *foie gras de canard* has opened a whole new horizon in cooking in this country, and American chefs have put their imaginations to work—sometimes with splendid results, sometimes in ways that would make a Gascon shudder. Because of its exceedingly delicate texture, fresh foie gras must be treated with utmost care. It can shrink alarmingly and lose flavor if handled or cooked in the wrong way—and at prices exceeding forty dollars a pound retail, that can be a horrifying experience.

CHOOSING AND HANDLING FOIE GRAS

A fresh duck foie gras typically weighs about twenty ounces, although it can weigh as much as two pounds. A quality liver is beige, smooth-textured, and slightly resilient to the touch. In general, choose small to medium size livers. The largest ones tend to shrink more while cooking. A fresh foie gras should have no off odor and no discoloration. Brown edges or white spots indicate that it is getting old—do not eat it. Pale bruises, however, are the natural consequence of rough handling and do not affect flavor. The shelf life of a fresh foie gras purchased in a vacuum package, as most are, is about a week. A cooked terrine, sealed in solidified fat, can be kept for up to four weeks in a refrigerator. Certain foie gras recipes—terrines and recipes involving steaming or roasting—call for deveining the liver. If the liver is to be sliced and sautéed, this procedure is not necessary.

Fresh foie gras comes in three official U.S. Department of Agriculture (USDA) grades, A, B, and C. A is considered the best because it has the fewest veins, thus more meat, and somewhat higher resistence to melting when cooked. This top grade can be used for everything from sautéeing and steaming to making terrines. The B grade has more veins. It also can be sautéed and steamed with good results, but in general it is used for terrines. The C grade, which is webbed with veins, is never sold at the retail level. It usually finds its way into processed mousses and terrines.

MARINADES

In France, foie gras is soaked in highly salted and iced milk or water for up to three hours in the refrigerator to extract the blood. The vacuum-packed American foie gras does not need soaking because most of the blood is removed during the packing process.

Marinades are made with Armagnac and spices. Strongly flavored liquids, however, tend to overwhelm the delicate liver's flavor. Sauternes, port, or other fortified wines are better suited because they mellow and sweeten the liver in a more subtle way.

DEVEINING FRESH FOIE GRAS

The purpose of deveining foie gras is to extract any residual red spots as well as leave the liver smooth-textured.

When deveining a foie gras, the liver should be at room temperature; if it is too cold, the liver is brittle and may break.

Foie Gras

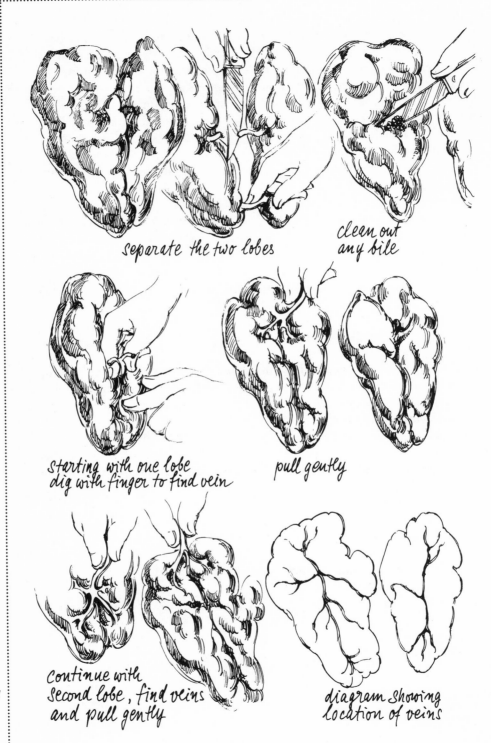

separate the two lobes

clean out
any bile

starting with one lobe
dig with finger to find vein

pull gently

continue with
second lobe, find veins
and pull gently

diagram showing
location of veins

1. A fresh duck liver somewhat resembles a small, deflated football. It has two lobes, one twice as large as the other; the surface is smooth and shiny. Before deveining, peel off any patches of translucent membrane that remain on the surface.

2. Gently pull apart the two lobes as illustrated. If they do not separate entirely, use a knife to sever the veins that hold them together. Inspect the area inside the folds. If any green bile spots appear, remove them with a knife. This is very important. If the bile remains it will give a bitter taste to the liver.

3. There are two sets of veins in a liver, one in each lobe. Find the thick, deep vein that runs through the center of the large lobe by gently digging into the liver with your fingertips as illustrated. Do not dig in too deeply or you might break the liver. When you locate the large vein, carefully pull it out as you follow it with your finger. It will have several branches that you should remove also.

4. The smaller lobe has a similar vein. Repeat the process to remove this. The liver is now ready for cooking.

PREPARING FOIE GRAS

Foie gras in this country is usually sliced and sautéed, or seasoned and baked in a terrine. As the recipes in this book illustrate, foie gras can be prepared in a much wider variety of ways. At the Daguin family restaurant in the Hôtel de France, it also is steamed and poached, and even added to soups, stews, and stuffings to lend a haunting echo of richness—in its own way, not unlike the effect of truffles, that other regal product of southwestern France. Some of the more imaginative, indeed whimsical, recipes that have been developed by André Daguin are foie gras baked in green pineapple (page 36); cured foie gras in coarse salt (page 37); papillote of foie gras with bay scallops (page 24); and clear pheasant broth holding cubes of foie gras (page 77).

Foie Gras

WARM FOIE GRAS

Foie Gras aux Poireaux et Oignons Verts

STEAMED FOIE GRAS WITH LEEKS AND SCALLIONS

1 whole foie gras, about 1¼
   pounds, at room temperature
Salt and freshly ground white
   pepper to taste
2 tablespoons unsalted butter

8 large leeks, thinly sliced
2 teaspoons sherry vinegar
16 scallions
Coarse salt
1 tablespoon chopped chervil

Clean and devein the foie gras according to the instructions on page 7. Season the liver all over with salt and pepper.

Heat the butter in a small frying pan over a medium flame. Add the sliced leeks, sprinkle with salt and pepper, and cook, covered, for 30 minutes, or until the leeks appear puréed. Do not brown. Stir in the vinegar just before serving.

Meanwhile, place the foie gras in the top part of a *couscoussier* or a steamer along with the scallions. Steam for 20 minutes. Place the foie gras on a clean towel and cut it into ½-inch slices.

To serve, arrange two scallions and some leek purée on each warmed serving plate and top with one or two slices of foie gras, depending on the size. Sprinkle the liver with some coarse salt and chervil. Serve immediately. [*Yield: 8 servings*]

COUSCOUSSIER: a tall steamer in which couscous is usually cooked. The fact that the steamer part is large and far enough from the water makes it ideal to steam large pieces of meat such as *confit*.

*Warm
Foie Gras*

Foie Gras à l'Ananas Vert

SAUTÉED FOIE GRAS WITH GREEN PINEAPPLE

In this recipe use an unripe pineapple. The fruit will become slightly caramelized because of its sugar content, yet have a tart quality reinforced by the vinegar.

1 whole foie gras, about 1½ pounds, at room temperature
Salt and freshly ground white pepper to taste
¾ cup cubed (¼ inch by ¼ inch) unripe pineapple

2 tablespoons red wine vinegar
6 tablespoons unsalted butter, cut into small pieces

Remove the thin membrane around the liver and dry. Cut into 1-inch-thick slices. Season the liver slices all over with salt and pepper.

Heat a large frying pan over a high flame and cook the foie gras slices for 30 seconds on each side; they will be medium rare. Remove from the pan and keep on a paper towel in a warm place.

Add the pineapple cubes to the fat in the pan and sauté them over medium-high heat until they become golden and start to caramelize. Set aside in a warm place until ready to serve.

Discard the fat from the pan and deglaze the pan with the vinegar. Whisk in the butter pieces a few at a time until smooth and well incorporated. To serve, place the liver slices on warmed serving plates, garnish with the pineapple cubes, and spoon some sauce over each.   [*Yield: 8 servings*]

Foie Gras aux Zestes de Citron et Pamplemousse

STEAMED FOIE GRAS WITH LEMON AND GRAPEFRUIT ZESTS

1 whole foie gras, about 1¼
    pounds, at room temperature
Salt and freshly ground white
    pepper to taste
Zest of 1 lemon

Zest of a small grapefruit
⅓ cup port
¼ cup Armagnac
1 cup chicken stock
3 tablespoons heavy cream

Clean and devein the foie gras according to the instructions on page 7. Season the liver all over with salt and pepper.

Cut the lemon and grapefruit zests into a very fine julienne. Place in a small saucepan, cover with water, and bring to a boil. Blanch for 5 minutes. Drain and cool under cold running water.

Place the blanched lemon and grapefruit zests in a heavy saucepan and add the port and Armagnac. Warm over medium heat and flambé. Be careful because Armagnac can create high flames. When the flames disappear, reduce the liquid over high heat until it has nearly evaporated. Add the chicken stock and reduce by half.

Meanwhile, place the foie gras in the top part of a *couscoussier* or a steamer. Steam for 20 minutes. Place the foie gras on a paper towel on a warmed platter and keep warm.

Add the cream to the saucepan and reduce over high heat until the sauce slightly thickens. Slice the foie gras into serving portions, sprinkle with salt, and spoon the sauce over the slices. Serve immediately.   [*Yield: 8 servings*]

Foie Gras au Malaga, Madeire, ou Banyuls

FOIE GRAS BRAISED IN MALAGA, MADEIRA, OR BANYULS WINE

This recipe can be made with a variety of fortified wines, depending on the flavor and sweetness you want. Madeira, which ranges from relatively light and dry to dark and heavy bodied, is widely available in this country. Banyuls, an excellent fortified sweet wine from the Pyrenees region in southern France, somewhat like port, is available in limited quantities in the United States; if you cannot find it, port wine is a good substitute. Malaga, from the Mediterranean coast of Spain, ranges in flavor from semisweet (semidulce) to the thick and syrupy lagrima.

When serving the foie gras, make sure not to slice it in its sauce. The fat from the liver will run into the sauce and ruin it. Instead, slice it on paper towels, arrange the slices on platters, and spoon the sauce over them.

1 whole foie gras, about 1½ pounds, at room temperature
Salt and freshly ground white pepper to taste
2 large shallots, minced

2 cups dry Madeira, Banyuls, Port, or Malaga wine
1 4-ounce can truffles in their juice (optional)
¼ cup heavy cream

Clean and devein the foie gras according to the instructions on page 7. Sprinkle the liver all over with salt and pepper.

Place the foie gras in a heavy-gauge saucepan that is just large enough to hold the foie gras, but not much larger or the sauce will burn. Add the shallots and the wine of your choice, cover, and place the saucepan over high heat. When the wine is hot, flambé. When the flame dies, add the truffle juice, if desired, cover, and cook for 20 minutes over medium heat. Remove the foie gras from the saucepan, place it on a clean towel or paper towels, and keep warm while making the sauce.

Using a spoon, skim off most of the fat on top of the cooking liquid and add the cream to the saucepan. Reduce the sauce to a thick consistency over high heat—about a minute. Slice the truffles into thin sticks and add them to the pot. Adjust seasonings to taste.

Slice the foie gras into serving portions, then arrange on individual plates. Spoon the sauce over the slices and serve immediately. [*Yield: 8 to 10 servings*]

Foie Gras aux Choux Saisis Vinaigrés

FOIE GRAS IN CABBAGE LEAVES

1 whole foie gras, about $1\frac{1}{4}$
  pounds, at room temperature
Salt and freshly ground white
  pepper to taste
10 large tender green cabbage
  leaves

10 tablespoons rendered duck fat
  (see recipe page 176)
Coarse salt to taste
5 teaspoons red wine vinegar

Clean and devein the foie gras according to the instructions on page 7. Sprinkle the liver all over with salt and pepper.

Place the foie gras in the top part of a *couscoussier* or a steamer. Steam for 15 minutes.

Meanwhile, remove the hard core at the base of the cabbage leaves and blanch the leaves in salted boiling water for 5 minutes. Drain and dry thoroughly with paper towels. Place the leaves on an oven rack over the sink.

In a small saucepan, bring the duck fat to the smoking point over high heat. Drizzle each cabbage leaf with 1 tablespoon of fat. Be careful; the leaves will sizzle and smoke.

Cut the foie gras into ten slices and arrange each one at the center of a cabbage leaf. Sprinkle each slice with a pinch of coarse salt and $\frac{1}{2}$ teaspoon of vinegar. Fold the edges of the leaves over the foie gras to form small packages.

Preheat the broiler.

Arrange the packages on a baking sheet and place under the broiler for 3 minutes, or until the leaves start to brown. Serve immediately.   [*Yield: 10 servings*]

Escalopes de Foie Gras Sautées aux Radis

SAUTÉED FOIE GRAS WITH RADISHES

32 small radishes, trimmed
1 whole foie gras, about 1¼
   pounds, at room temperature
2 tablespoons unsalted butter (if
   necessary)

1 large shallot, minced
2 tablespoons dry Madeira wine
1 cup chicken stock
Salt and freshly ground white
   pepper to taste

Bring a pot of lightly salted water to a boil. Blanch the radishes for 8 minutes. Drain and plunge into ice water to stop the cooking. Drain again and set aside until ready to use.

Remove any membrane on the liver and dry. Cut into 1-inch-thick slices. Heat a large frying pan over a medium-high flame and sauté the slices for about 30 seconds on each side. Remove from the pan and place on a paper towel on a platter. Keep warm.

Discard the fat from the pan if it is burned; add 2 tablespoons butter, if necessary. Reduce the heat to medium-low and sauté the radishes for about 4 minutes, or until they are cooked through. Remove from the pan and put between two paper towels to absorb the fat.

Add the shallot to the pan and deglaze with the Madeira. Bring to a boil over high heat and add the chicken stock. Bring to a boil and reduce by half. Add the radishes to the pan to warm them through. Arrange the liver slices on warmed serving plates and spoon the sauce over them. Arrange a few radishes on each plate and serve immediately.   [*Yield: 8 to 10 servings*]

Foie Gras Escalopé aux Épinards

SAUTÉED FOIE GRAS WITH SPINACH

*1 whole foie gras, about 1¼
pounds, at room temperature
36 spinach leaves, rinsed and
thoroughly dried*

*Salt and freshly ground white
pepper to taste*

Remove the thin membrane around the liver and dry. Cut into slices about
1¼ inches thick.

Heat a large frying pan over medium-high flame and sauté the foie gras
slices for about 30 seconds on one side. Turn the slices and add the spinach
to the pan. Cover and cook for another minute.

Remove the liver slices from the pan and place on a paper towel. Season
with salt and pepper. Continue cooking the spinach, if necessary, until
wilted. Divide the spinach among six warmed serving plates and top with
a slice of foie gras.   [*Yield: 8 to 10 servings*]

*Warm
Foie Gras*

19

Foie Gras aux Endives

BRAISED FOIE GRAS WITH ENDIVES

6 large endives
1 whole foie gras, about 1½
   pounds

Salt and freshly ground white
   pepper to taste
½ teaspoon sugar (optional)

Trim and rinse the endives. Slice them crosswise into thin strips.

Clean and devein the foie gras according to the instructions on page 7. Season the liver all over with salt and pepper.

Choose a nonaluminum pot that is large enough to hold the foie gras. Place the sliced endives at the bottom of the pot with a tablespoon of water. Cover tightly and cook over medium heat for 5 minutes, or until the endives start to wilt. Add the foie gras, cover, and cook for 20 minutes.

Remove the liver from the pot and place on paper towels. Keep warm. Strain the endives to discard the fat and put them back into the pot. Cook over high heat until they start to turn golden and caramelize slightly. If the endives are too bitter for your taste or if you desire to have a sweet-and-sour flavor, add the sugar to the pot. Strain again, if necessary.

To serve, slice the liver into individual portions and arrange on warmed serving plates. Sprinkle with salt, garnish with the endives, and serve immediately.   [*Yield: 8 to 10 servings*]

Foie Gras à l'Armagnac

FOIE GRAS COOKED IN ARMAGNAC

Armagnac adds a wonderful accent to many dishes, but be careful when using it to flambé, it can produce high flames. If the flames become too high, cover the pot immediately to snuff them out.

For this recipe it is essential to use a pot that is just large enough to hold the liver, no bigger. If the pot is too large, the juices will evaporate rapidly and the liver might burn before it is cooked.

1 whole foie gras, about 1½ pounds, at room temperature
Salt and freshly ground white pepper to taste

1½ cups Armagnac
½ cup chicken stock
Coarse salt

Clean and devein the foie gras according to the instructions on page 7. Season the liver all over with salt and pepper.

Place the liver in a deep, heavy pot that is just large enough to hold it. Pour the Armagnac over the liver, bring to a boil over high heat, and then flambé. When the alcohol is completely burned off, the flames will die and only the flavor of the Armagnac will remain. Cover the pot and cook for 20 minutes over medium heat, making sure the liquid does not evaporate.

When the foie gras is cooked, remove it from the pot and drain on paper towels. Keep warm. Add the chicken stock to the pot and reduce it over high heat by a third. Slice the foie gras into serving portions and arrange on a serving platter. Spoon the sauce over it. Serve immediately with coarse salt on the side.   [*Yield: 8 servings*]

*Warm
Foie Gras*

Foie Gras aux Raisins Verts

FOIE GRAS WITH GREEN GRAPES

1 whole foie gras, about 1¼
  pounds, at room temperature
Salt and freshly ground white
  pepper to taste
2 pounds seedless green grapes,
  not too ripe, rinsed

¼ cup port wine
1 cup dry white wine
1 cup duck stock or chicken stock
3 tablespoons heavy cream

Clean and devein the foie gras according to the instructions on page 7. Season the liver all over with salt and pepper.

Select forty-two large, unblemished grapes for the garnish. Peel them (if you cannot get seedless grapes, remove the seeds with a needle). Do not crush the grapes. Place them in a bowl and marinate in the port for 1 hour, or until ready to use. Drain and reserve the grapes and the port separately.

Remove the remaining grapes from their stems and place in a saucepan large enough to hold the grapes and the foie gras. Crush the grapes lightly with a wooden spoon to extract their juice. Add the port and white wine to the saucepan and place the liver on top of the grapes, but do not immerse in the liquid. The vapors of the wine and grape juice will steam the liver. Cover tightly and cook over medium-high heat for 20 minutes. Remove the liver from the pan and place it on paper towels. Keep warm.

Using a spoon skim off most of the fat on top of the cooking liquid. Add the stock to the saucepan and cook for 5 minutes over high heat. Pass the sauce through a fine sieve, pushing on the grapes to extract all of the juice, and return the strained sauce to the saucepan. Add the cream to the saucepan, bring to a boil, and cook for 1 minute. Add the remaining whole grapes and boil just to warm them. Meanwhile, slice the foie gras. Spoon some sauce onto warmed serving plates and arrange a slice of foie gras on top. Garnish with the warmed grapes and serve immediately.   [*Yield: 8 to 10 servings*]

Foie Gras aux Deux Olives

STEAMED FOIE GRAS WITH GREEN AND BLACK OLIVES

1 whole foie gras, about 1¼
    pounds, at room temperature
Salt and freshly ground white
    pepper to taste
48 green olives, cured in brine,
    pitted

48 black olives, cured in brine,
    pitted
¼ cup heavy cream

Clean and devein the foie gras according to the instructions on page 7. Season the liver all over with salt and pepper.

Place the foie gras in the top part of a *couscoussier* or a steamer. Steam for 20 minutes.

Meanwhile, place the green and black olives in separate saucepans. Cover each with cold water and bring to a boil. Blanch the olives for 5 minutes. Drain. Reserve sixteen olives of each color for the garnish. Place the remaining green olives in the bowl of a food processor or a blender with 2 tablespoons of cream. Purée until smooth and set aside. Repeat with the black olives. Season both olive mixtures with pepper.

When the foie gras is cooked, transfer it to paper towels. Poach the reserved olives in the water of the steamer just to warm them. Slice the foie gras into eight serving portions. Spoon some of the two olive purées onto warmed serving plates and arrange a slice of foie gras on top. Garnish with the whole olives and serve immediately.   [*Yield: 8 servings*]

*Warm
Foie Gras*

Papillotes de Foie Gras et de Petoncles

PAPILLOTES OF FOIE GRAS AND BAY SCALLOPS

1 whole foie gras, about 1¼
   pounds, at room temperature
Salt and freshly ground white
   pepper to taste
32 bay scallops
¼ cup heavy cream

¼ cup dry vermouth
1 leek, white part only, finely
   julienned
3 tender celery stalks, finely
   julienned

Remove the thin membrane around the liver and dry. Cut into eight slices about 1¼-inch thick. Season all over with salt and pepper. Heat a large nonstick frying pan over a high flame. Quickly sauté the foie gras slices, 30 seconds on each side. Remove them from the pan and drain them on paper towels.

Pour off the fat from the pan. Add the scallops to the pan and sauté quickly for 30 seconds over high heat. Place half of the scallops in a blender or the bowl of a food processor along with the cream and the vermouth. Puree to a smooth paste.

Form eight double-layered 20- by 12-inch aluminum foil rectangles. Arrange one rectangle on a work surface with a short side parallel to the edge of the counter. Spoon some of the scallop paste onto the center of the lower half. Top with a slice of foie gras, two scallops and some of the julienned leek and celery. Season with salt and pepper. Fold the top of the aluminum foil back over the ingredients and crimp the sides to enclose the food and form a secure papillote. Repeat with the remaining ingredients. This can be done ahead of time. (If you refrigerate the papillotes, make sure they are completely cool before doing so. The temperature difference between the food inside of the pouch and the cool refrigerator outside might cause bacteria to develop. Remove the papillotes from the refrigerator half an hour before cooking.)

Preheat the oven to 450 degrees.

Arrange the papillotes on a baking sheet and cook for 8 minutes. Serve immediately.   [*Yield: 8 servings*]

NOTE: In this recipe the scallops can be substituted for salmon or one pound of lobster meat.

COLD FOIE GRAS

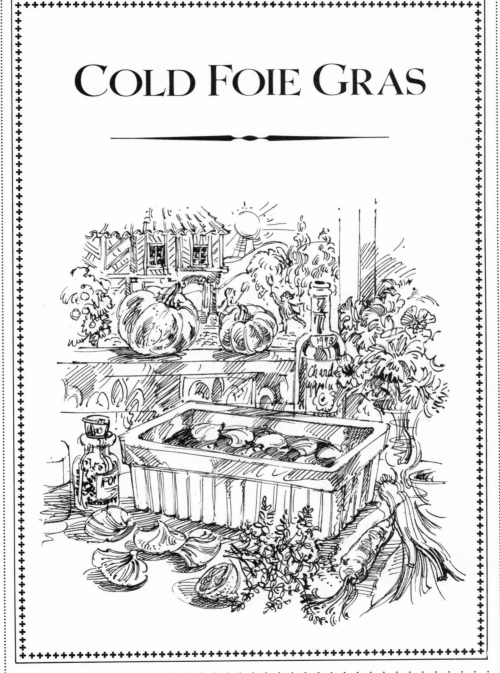

$\mathcal{T}$o make a foie gras terrine you should use a standard five-cup terrine mold with a heavy lid. The lid should not have a handle because after cooking it is reversed and used to compress the foie gras and extract the excess fat. An alternative is a five-cup, stainless-steel rectangular cake mold. In this case, line the bottom and sides of the mold with plastic wrap, leaving a five-inch overhang on all sides. Place the uncooked foie gras in the mold and fold the wrap over it. Cook as directed. After cooking, cut a piece of cardboard to the size of the mold, wrap it in several layers of plastic, and place it on top of the liver. Put some heavy cans on top of the cardboard to compress the foie gras and extract the excess fat.

When cooking a terrine, the oven temperature should not exceed 200 degrees. The foie gras should cook at a low, even temperature to avoid shrinkage. The cooking times in the following recipes should be used as guidelines; they represent the minimum amount of cooking needed. The timing may vary according to the quality of the foie gras and its temperature when placed in the oven. Invest in a small meat thermometer. The foie gras is cooked when the internal temperature reaches 115 to 120 degrees.

Plan to cook the terrine *at least three days before serving*. This time is important to allow the flavors to mellow.

Season the foie gras generously with salt and pepper before cooking or the terrine will be bland.

Terrine de Foie Gras Nature

TERRINE OF DUCK FOIE GRAS

1 whole foie gras, about 1½ pounds, at room temperature

Salt and freshly crushed white pepper to taste

Preheat the oven to 200 degrees.

Bring a large pot of salted water to a rolling boil. Meanwhile, clean and devein the liver according to the instructions on page 7. Blanch the foie gras in the boiling water for 2 minutes. Remove from the pot and pat dry with paper towels. Season the liver all over with salt and white pepper.

Place the foie gras in a five-cup terrine mold and cover (see notes on molds page 27). In a deep ovenproof pan, layer six paper towels on top of one another to form a thick stock, place the mold on top of them. Fill the pan with boiling water, halfway up the sides of the mold. The paper towels will absorb the water and create a *bain-marie* since all sides of the mold will be in contact with water. Place the pan in the oven and cook for 40 minutes, or until the internal temperature of the liver reaches 115 degrees.

Remove from the oven and place the terrine in a pan filled with ice water. Reverse the mold cover to exert light pressure on the liver. This will force enough fat to the surface to cover the liver. If the terrine you are using does not have a cover or the cover has a handle, cut a rectangle the size of the mold out of a piece of cardboard. Wrap it in several layers of plastic wrap. Place it on top of the liver and weigh it down with two small cans. When the foie gras is entirely covered by the fat, remove the cardboard, cover tightly, and refrigerate for at least two to three days before serving. The liver will keep up to three weeks if kept refrigerated under its layer of fat.

To serve, remove the fat from the surface, unmold, and cut into serving slices.   [*Yield: 10 servings*]

Terrine de Foie Gras au Sauternes

TERRINE OF DUCK FOIE GRAS AND SAUTERNES

1 whole foie gras, about 1½
    pounds, at room temperature
⅔ cup Sauternes

Salt and freshly ground white
    pepper to taste

Clean and devein the liver according to the instructions on page 7. Season the liver all over with salt and pepper.

Place the foie gras in a four-cup terrine mold (see notes on molds, page 27). Pour the Sauternes over the foie gras and refrigerate, covered, for two hours.

Thirty minutes before cooking the terrine, remove it from the refrigerator and preheat the oven to 200 degrees.

In a deep ovenproof pan, layer six paper towels on top of one another to form a thick stock, and place the mold on top of them. Fill the pan with boiling water, halfway up the sides of the mold. Place the pan in the oven and cook for 40 minutes, or until the internal temperature of the liver reaches 115 degrees.

Remove from the oven and place the terrine in a pan filled with ice water. Reverse the mold cover to exert a light pressure on the liver. This will force enough fat to the surface to cover the liver. If the terrine you are using does not have a cover or the cover has a handle, cut a rectangle the size of the mold out of a piece of cardboard. Wrap it in several layers of plastic wrap. Place it on top of the liver and weight it down with two small cans. When the foie gras is entirely covered by the fat, remove the cardboard, cover tightly, and refrigerate for at least two or three days before serving.

To serve, remove the fat from the surface, unmold, and cut into serving slices. [*Yield: 10 servings*]

*Cold Foie
Gras*

Foie Gras Poché au Chardonnay

FOIE GRAS POACHED IN CHARDONNAY

3 cups dry Chardonnay wine
2 cups water
1 onion pierced with 3 cloves
1 garlic clove
1 carrot, chopped
$\frac{1}{2}$ teaspoon thyme
8 black peppercorns

Salt to taste
1 whole foie gras, about $1\frac{1}{2}$
    pounds, at room temperature
Freshly ground white pepper to
    taste
Juice of 1 lemon

For this recipe, use a deep, enamel or copper pot. Do not use aluminum because it will discolor the foie gras.

To make a court bouillon combine the Chardonnay, water, onion, garlic, carrot, thyme, and peppercorns in the pot. Bring to a boil and simmer for 15 minutes. Lightly salt the court bouillon. Meanwhile, clean and devein the foie gras according to the instructions on page 7. Season the liver all over with salt and pepper. Add the foie gras to the court bouillon and simmer for 20 minutes.

Transfer the liver to a glass or porcelain dish just large enough to hold it. Strain the court bouillon through a fine sieve and pour over the liver to cover. The liver will finish cooking as it cools. The fat of the liver will rise to the surface and form an airtight seal under which the liver can be kept for several days in the refrigerator.

When ready to eat the foie gras, remove and place the fat in a blender with the juice of a lemon. Blend thoroughly. Spread this mixture on country-style French bread; it makes a wonderful hors d'oeuvre accompanied by a glass of Chardonnay. Remove the liver from the court bouillon, pat dry, and cut into serving slices.   [*Yield: 10 servings*]

Foie Gras Chemisé de Poireaux

FOIE GRAS WRAPPED IN LEEKS

4 large tender leeks, green parts
   only
1 whole foie gras, about $1\frac{1}{4}$
   pounds, at room temperature

Salt and freshly ground white
   pepper to taste

Two or three days before you plan to serve the foie gras, trim the leeks, remove and discard the tough outer leaves (or save for stock), and separate the tender inner leaves. Rinse the inner leaves thoroughly, then blanch in well-salted water for 2 minutes. Drain and plunge immediately into ice water to keep the leeks green. Drain again and dry well. Preheat the oven to 200 degrees.

Line the bottom and the sides of a five-cup rectangular mold (see notes on molds page 27) with the leek leaves, reserving enough to cover the top of the liver. The leaves should overlap one another; no liver should be exposed when you unmold it.

Clean and devein the foie gras according to the instructions on page 7. Season the liver all over with salt and pepper. Place it in the prepared mold and layer the reserved leek leaves on top. Cover.

In a deep ovenproof pan, layer six paper towels on top of one another to form a thick stock, and place the mold on top of them. Fill the pan with boiling water, halfway up the sides of the mold. Place in the oven for 50 minutes, or until the internal temperature of the liver reaches 115 degrees.

Remove the terrine mold from the oven and place it in a pan filled with ice water to cool. Reverse the mold lid to exert slight pressure on the liver. This will force enough fat to the surface to cover the liver. If the terrine you are using does not have a cover or the cover has a handle, cut a rectangle the size of the mold out of a piece of cardboard. Wrap it in several layer of plastic wrap. Place it on top of the liver and weigh it down with two small cans. When the foie gras is entirely covered by the fat, remove the cardboard, cover tightly, and refrigerate for at least two to three days before serving. The liver will keep up to three weeks if kept refrigerated under its layer of fat.

To serve, remove the fat from the surface, invert the terrine on a serving platter, and slice. [*Yield: 10 servings*]

Foie Gras aux Pleurottes

FOIE GRAS AND OYSTER MUSHROOMS TERRINE

$\frac{1}{4}$ cup rendered duck fat (see
   recipe page 176)
1 pound oyster mushrooms
Salt and freshly ground white
   pepper to taste

1 whole foie gras, about $1\frac{1}{2}$
   pounds, at room temperature

Three to four days before you plan to serve the foie gras, heat the duck fat in a frying pan to the smoking point. Sauté the mushrooms for 10 minutes, or until all their liquid has evaporated. Drain on paper towels. Season the mushrooms with salt and pepper, and line the sides and the bottom of a five-cup terrine mold with them (see notes on molds page 27), reserving some to cover the top of the liver.

Preheat the oven to 200 degrees.

Clean and devein the foie gras according to the instructions on page 7. Season the liver all over with salt and pepper. Place the foie gras in the terrine. Cover with the remaining mushrooms. Cover with a lid or plastic wrap (see note on mold, page 27). In a deep ovenproof pan, layer six paper towels on top of one another to form a thick stock; place the mold on top of them. Fill the pan with boiling water, halfway up the sides. Place the pan in the oven and cook for 50 minutes, or until the internal temperature of the liver reaches 115 degrees.

Remove from the oven and place the mold in a pan filled with ice water to cool. Reverse the mold cover to exert light pressure on the liver. This will force enough fat to the surface to cover the liver. If the terrine you are using does not have a cover or the cover has a handle, cut a rectangle the size of the mold out of a piece of cardboard. Wrap it in several layers of plastic wrap. Place it on top of the liver and weigh it down with two small cans.

When the foie gras is entirely covered by the fat, remove the cardboard, cover tightly, and refrigerate for at least two to three days before serving. The liver will keep up to three weeks if kept refrigerated under its layer of fat. When ready to serve, remove the fat from the surface and unmold. Slice and serve with a sweet wine such as Sauternes. [*Yield: 8 to 10 servings*]

Foie Gras aux Épinards

FOIE GRAS AND SPINACH TERRINE

2 pounds spinach
¾ cup heavy cream
Salt and freshly ground white
    pepper to taste

1 whole foie gras, about 1½
    pounds, at room temperature

Clean the spinach leaves and discard the stems. Bring a large pot of salted water to a boil, add the spinach leaves, and blanch for two minutes. Drain well and cool. When cool enough to handle, squeeze out as much water as possible.

In a small saucepan, bring the cream to a boil. Place the spinach and the hot cream in the bowl of a food processor and purée until smooth. Season with salt and pepper to taste. Clean and devein the foie gras according to the instructions on page 7. Season the liver all over with salt and pepper.

Preheat the oven to 200 degrees.

Place the foie gras in a five-cup terrine mold (see note on molds page 27).

Pour the spinach mixture over the liver, making sure the liver is completely covered. In a deep ovenproof pan, layer six paper towels on top of one another to form a thick stock; place the mold on top of them. Fill the pan with boiling water, halfway up the sides. Place the pan in the oven and cook for 1⅓ hours, or until the internal temperature of the foie gras reaches 115 degrees. Remove the terrine from the oven and place it in a pan of iced water to cool.

Reverse the mold cover to exert light pressure on the liver. This will force enough fat to the surface to cover the liver. If the terrine you are using does not have a cover or the cover has a handle, cut a rectangle the size of the mold out of a piece of cardboard. Wrap it in several layers of plastic wrap. Place it on top of the liver and weigh it down with two small cans. When the foie gras is entirely covered by the fat, remove the cardboard, cover tightly, and refrigerate. This terrine should be eaten within two days of cooking as aging does not improve it. To serve, unmold the terrine and slice. Serve with lightly toasted country-style French bread. [*Yield: 10 servings*]

Le Foie Gras Gelé au Torchon

FOIE GRAS CURED AND FROZEN

This unusual method of preparing foie gras gives the liver a dry, firm texture. The prepared liver might show some brown spots from the coarse salt treatment. If it does, simply remove them with a knife.

1 whole foie gras, about 1¼ pounds, at room temperature
2 cups coarse salt

½ cup freshly ground white pepper to taste

Ten days before serving the foie gras, clean and devein it according to the instructions on page 7.

Place the liver at one end of a large clean cotton kitchen towel 30 by 20 inches, and roll it tightly for just one turn. Sprinkle the rest of the towel with salt and pepper, and continue rolling very tightly. Make sure the salt and pepper are evenly distributed.

To make a tight package, twist the overlapping ends of the towel firmly in opposite directions and tie them with kitchen string. Freeze the liver for eight days. Two days before serving, place the liver in the vegetable bin of the refrigerator.

Unwrap the liver 1 hour before serving but do not slice it. This should be done at the last moment. Slice the liver thinly and serve with lightly toasted country-style French bread.   [*Yield: 10 to 12 servings*]

Foie Gras,
Magret, and
Other Good Food
from Gascony

Foie Gras en Citrouille

FOIE GRAS IN PUMPKIN

This is a particularly festive way to prepare foie gras for parties.

1 whole foie gras, about 1¾
    pounds, at room temperature
Salt and freshly ground white
    pepper to taste

1 small pumpkin, 3 to 4 pounds
⅔ cup dry Madeira wine
Coarse salt

Clean and devein the foie gras according to the instructions on page 7. Season the liver all over with salt and pepper. Preheat the oven to 200 degrees.

Cut off the pumpkin top and remove the seeds and membrane from the cavity, being careful not to pierce the skin.

Pour the Madeira into the pumpkin shell and sprinkle with salt and pepper. Place the foie gras in the pumpkin, put the top back, and wrap in aluminum foil.

Pour a thick layer of coarse salt on a baking sheet and place the pumpkin on it upright. The salt will stabilize the pumpkin. Bake for 1½ hours or until the internal temperature reaches 115 degrees.

Remove the pumpkin from the oven and cool to room temperature. Refrigerate for 12 hours before serving. Scoop the foie gras out of the shell at the table and serve with lightly toasted country-style French bread. If the shell has no holes in it after the foie gras has been eaten, serve a pumpkin soup in it. The flavors from the shell will give a rich taste to the soup. [*Yield: 8 to 10 servings*]

*Cold Foie
Gras*

Foie Gras dans L'Ananas Vert

FOIE GRAS IN GREEN PINEAPPLE

*1 foie gras, about 1¾ pounds, at
   room temperature*
*Salt and freshly ground white
   pepper to taste*

*1 unripe pineapple, about 3¾
   pounds*
⅔ cup white rum
Coarse salt

Clean and devein the foie gras according to the instructions on page 7. Season the liver all over with salt and pepper.

Preheat the oven to 200 degrees.

Cut off the pineapple top and scoop out the flesh, leaving about 1 inch attached to the skin. Be careful not to pierce the skin.

Pour the rum into the pineapple shell and sprinkle with salt and pepper. Place the foie gras in the pineapple, put the top back, and wrap in aluminum foil.

Pour a thick layer of coarse salt on a baking sheet and place the pineapple on it upright. The salt will stabilize the pineapple. Bake for 1½ hours, or until the internal temperature reaches 115 degrees. Remove the pineapple from the oven and cool to room temperature.

Refrigerate for 12 hours before serving. Scoop the foie gras out of the pineapple at the table and serve with lightly toasted country-style French bread.   [*Yield: 8 to 10 servings*]

Foie Gras en Salaison

FOIE GRAS CURED IN SALT

This is a very easy recipe to make, but follow it carefully because the recipe does not allow for any variation.

1 foie gras, about 1½ pounds, at room temperature
Salt and freshly ground white pepper

6 cups coarse salt
1 cup freshly ground black pepper

Three days before serving the foie gras, clean and devein it according to the instructions on page 7. Season the liver all over with salt and white pepper.

Press the large lobe of the liver against the small lobe to form one large piece of foie gras—try to leave no space in between.

Place the liver at one end of a double layer of cheesecloth and roll it for four rotations to wrap well. Twist the overhanging ends firmly in opposite directions to secure tightly. Tie the ends with kitchen twine. A tightly wrapped foie gras will keep longer.

Combine the coarse salt with the black pepper in a mixing bowl. Cover the bottom of another mixing bowl with half of the mixture, place the foie gras on top, and cover with the remaining salt and pepper mixture. The foie gras should be completely buried under a ½-inch-thick layer of salt and pepper. Place a heavy weight on top of the foie gras and refrigerate for three days.

Before serving, remove the liver from the seasonings and unwrap it. It will be dark beige and may have some dark spots on the surface. These are caused by the salt but do not affect the flavor. For cosmetic reasons you may want to remove the dark spots with a knife. Slice the foie gras into ¼-inch-thick pieces and serve with some toasted country-style French bread.   [*Yield: 10 servings*]

CONFIT

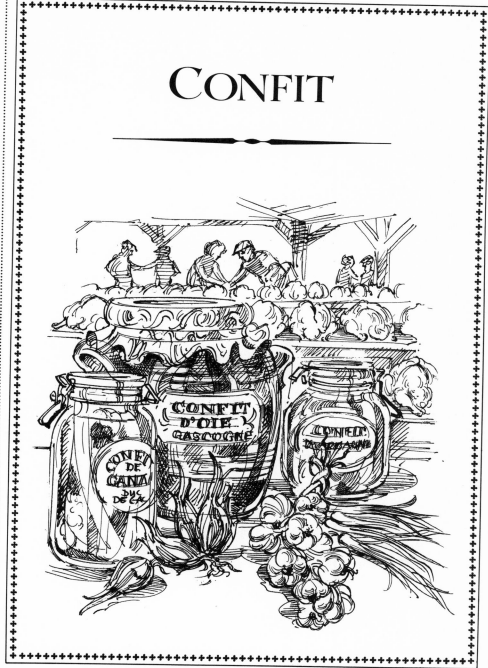

Confit is another glory of Gascon cooking. The term *confit* derives from the French *confire*, which means to preserve or to conserve. The process typically involves simmering meat in its own fat to lend an ineffable richness and succulence without being fatty, unlike any other method of cooking. The meat takes on a slightly salty and herb-saturated flavor, redolent of garlic, cloves, and other spices. The meat is then stored for months encased in its own solidified fat to ripen. The longer the meat is stored, the better the *confit* will be. In France a good *confit* is often ripened for up to two years.

The most common *confit* is made with fattened ducks *(confit de canard)* or fattened geese *(confit d'oie)*. The practice of making *confit* paralleled the introduction of foie gras in France. After the enlarged livers were removed from the ducks and geese the farmers found themselves with a surplus of meat that had to be either consumed quickly or preserved. Foie gras birds, it turned out, were ideal for preserving this way because they had so much fat under the skin.

On a fattened duck or goose virtually every part is edible. The liver is used for terrines and hot appetizers, the breast *(magret)* is best sautéed. The legs, wings, gizzards, and neck are usually cooked as confit. They can be eaten as is or added to various dishes such as cassoulet or *garbure,* a cabbage soup from the southwest of France. Even the carcass—with the legs, wings and breast removed—is delicious roasted or grilled. The residual meat on the carcass has a distinctly delicate and earthy flavor, owing to its contact with the liver. In Gascony, the carcasses of fattened ducks or geese are called *demoiselles.*

Aside from fattened duck and geese, other meats can be *"confit."* Pork and capon are frequently used in Gascony. And today, leaner meats such as rabbit, turkey, and squab are often treated this way—in these cases the fat from other animals, such as duck or pork, is used. The best sections of meat for *confit* are those that have the most fat and moisture, such a duck leg or shoulder of pork, as opposed to breast of duck or pork loin. The meat of a well-made *confit* should literally fall off the bone.

Certain root vegetables are also cooked *confit-*style to lend extra flavor, specifically garlic, shallots, and green onions.

Cloves

The word comes from the Latin *clavus* meaning "nail" and, indeed, the clove tree's unexpanded flower, when dried and hardened, looks like a little brown nail. Clove trees flourish near the sea and are cultivated in Indonesia, Zanzibar, Madigascar, and the Caribbean. Cloves are purported to be a potent aphrodisiac. While the proof is up to you, cloves can definitely be recommended as an effective antiseptic. The clove, which imparts to *confit* some of its aromatic pungency, also is an important ingredient in the preserving process. It will help the *confit* keep longer.

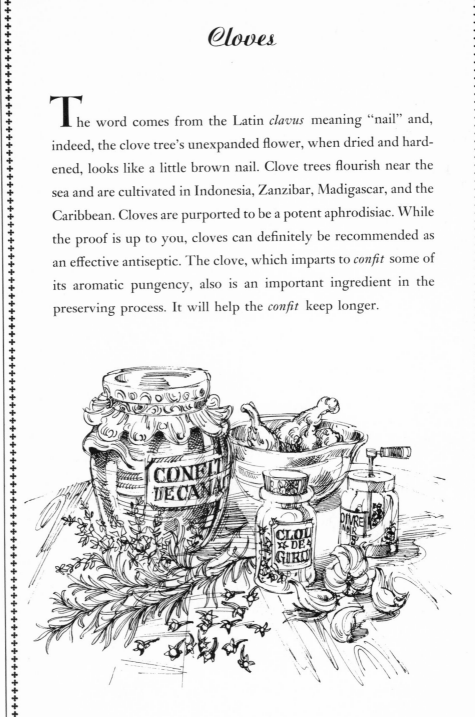

MOULARD AND PEKIN DUCKS

The moulard is the duck used in France to produce foie gras. It is a cross between the muscovy duck (in French known as the *Barbarie*) and the Pekin duck. Moulards are larger than the others, and have more assertive-flavored meat—it is not, however, at all gamey. Before the availability of moulard ducks in this country, the fatty Pekin ducks were used to make *confit.* They are smaller than moulards, have a slightly thinner skin and a lighter flesh. They make an acceptable *confit,* though—the major difference is that *confit* made with Pekin ducks is slightly dryer than *confit* made with moulards.

Although today moulard ducks are sold in specialty stores and some supermarkets (see Shopping Sources, page 189), the recipes in this book have been devised for both moulards and Pekins. As individual recipes explain, some adjustment needs to be made when using Pekins.

Moulard ducks should not be confused with mallard ducks, which are very lean wild ducks.

MAKING CONFIT

Making *confit* is a three-step process. First, the meat is rubbed with salt, herbs, and spices, then stored in a container, in the refrigerator from several hours to a few days, depending on the size and density of the meat. The salt extracts the moisture from the meat. This step is very important: the less moisture left on the meat, the longer the *confit* will keep.

The second stage is the cooking. The meat is placed in a deep, heavy-gauge pot and covered with rendered fat. (Gascon cooks traditionally use heavy-gauge copper pots because they distribute heat most evenly and efficiently.) The meat is then cooked over low heat for anywhere from one to three hours, depending on the type of meat. The fat should never become too hot; it should just gently simmer. If the fat gets too hot, the meat will fry, thus becoming dry and stringy. Slow cooking imparts a unique, buttery texture and rich flavor.

The third stage is storage. When the meat is thoroughly cooked it can be placed in sterilized mason jars and covered with a layer of strained, melted cooking fat. In Gascony, *confit* is often stored in deep two-handled earthenware containers. *Confit* is best if aged for at least a week in a cool place; properly made *confit* can be kept for three to four months. To assure an absolutely airtight seal, some cooks pour vegetable oil over the top of the solidified fat. Once the fat seal is broken, *confit* should be consumed within two days.

Before serving *confit,* remove the storage container from the refrigerator and set it out at room temperature for one to two hours so the fat softens.

Remove the meat from the container and scrape off the excess fat. Traditionally, *confit* is reheated in a heavy skillet in a small amount of fat until the skin becomes crisp and golden brown. Another good method is to reheat the *confit* in a steamer or *couscoussier* to remove some of the saltiness and fat, and then, at the last minute, place the meat under a broiler to crisp it. *Confit* is delicious on its own, perhaps with thinly sliced potatoes sautéed in a little duck fat from the *confit* jar; it is also a superb addition to soups, stews or cold in salad.

HOW TO CUT A DUCK

1. Place the duck breast side up on a cutting board. Locate the wishbone near the neck of the bird. Run a knife between the wishbone and the breast to cut through the skin and the flesh. Pull the bone with your hand to break it away from the carcass.

2. Cut through the skin and the flesh along the ridge of the breast bone. Starting on one side, run the knife between the bone and the flesh, scraping and pulling the meat. Cut through the joint of the shoulder to release the wing from the carcass. Cut through the fat and the skin to separate the wing from the magret. Repeat on the other side.

3. Trim the magret by cutting as much skin and fat as possible from around the meat. Pull out any vein that might be on the magret.

4. Run the knife through the joint between the legs and the carcass to detach them. Trim off the excess fat from the legs.

5. Reserve all the fat and skin trimming and remove all the excess from the carcass. It will be used for the rendered fat.

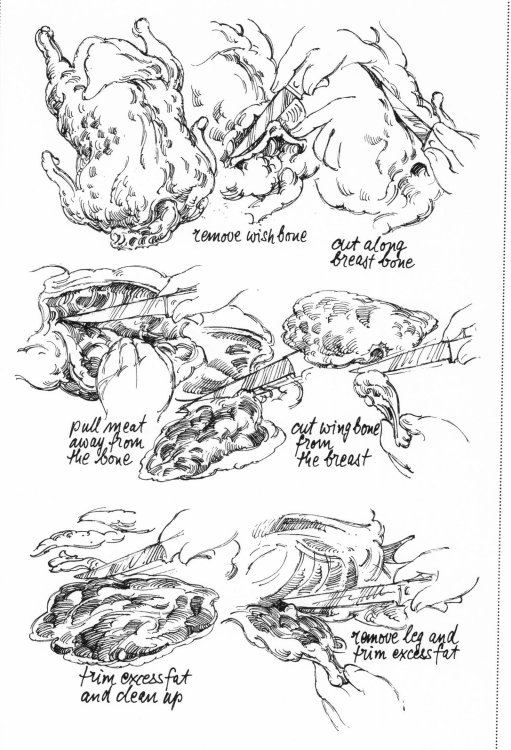

remove wish bone

cut along breast bone

pull meat away from the bone

cut wing bone from the breast

trim excess fat and clean up

remove leg and trim excess fat

Confit de Canard

DUCK CONFIT

IF USING MOULARD DUCKS:

2 moulard ducks, about 7 pounds each

4½ tablespoons coarse salt

1 tablespoon freshly ground black pepper

1½ teaspoons thyme

1½ teaspoons crushed rosemary

1 bay leaf, crushed

1 teaspoon quatre épices (see recipe page 175)

10 cloves

1 large garlic head, peeled

8 cups rendered duck fat (see recipe page 176)

IF USING PEKIN DUCKS:

2 Pekin ducks, about 5 pounds each

3 tablespoons coarse salt

1 tablespoon freshly ground black pepper

¾ teaspoon thyme

¾ teaspoon crushed rosemary

1 bay leaf, crushed

½ teaspoon quatre épices (see recipe page 175)

8 cloves

1 garlic head, peeled

6 cups rendered duck fat (see recipe page 176)

Vegetable oil, optional

At least a week before you wish to serve the confit, cut the ducks into serving pieces: the two legs with thighs attached, the two breasts, and wings (see illustration page 45). Cut off the wing tips and reserve them for later use. Save the two breasts for a magret recipe (see pages 59–67). Remove any excess of skin and fat from the carcasses, and set aside to make rendered fat (see page 176).

Place the duck legs and the wings in a large mixing bowl. Combine the salt, pepper, thyme, rosemary, bay leaf, and *quatre épices*. Rub the pieces all over with the mixture. Pierce the garlic with the cloves and bury them in between the duck pieces. Cover the bowl and refrigerate for 24 hours. The next day, melt the rendered duck fat in a large, heavy casserole such as an enamel cast-iron pot over medium heat.

Remove the duck pieces from the refrigerator and wipe off the herb and salt mixture. Reserve the garlic with the cloves. If the herbs are hard to remove, rinse the duck pieces very briefly under cold water. Dry thoroughly.

When the fat is warm but not hot, add the duck pieces to the pot along with the garlic cloves and cloves. Cook slowly over low heat for 3 hours for the legs of the moulard duck and $2\frac{1}{4}$ hours for the one of the Pekin duck, or until the meat can be easily be pierced with a straw or toothpick. The wings will take about 2 hours. The fat should never be boiling or the meat will fry. Ideally, the meat should cook with the fat at a constant low simmer. When the meat is cooked, remove the pieces from the pot and set them aside.

To store the *confit*, use tall glass jars or heavy crocks with wide openings. Fill the containers with boiling water, pour it out, and let dry. Arrange the duck pieces in the jars.

Pass the duck fat through a very fine sieve and pour it over the duck pieces. The duck should be completely covered by the fat; no pieces should stick out. Cover. Cool to room temperature, then refrigerate.

If you plan to store the *confit* for an extended time, cover the solid fat with a $\frac{1}{2}$-inch layer of vegetable oil to form an airtight seal that will keep the *confit* longer. Refrigerate for at least a week before eating; it can keep up to three months.

When ready to use, remove the pot from the refrigerator and let it stand at room temperature for several hours, or until the fat softens. Remove the pieces and wipe off the excess fat. The duck is then ready to use in the following recipes. Do not discard the fat; it can be used for cooking. [*Yield: 4 legs and 4 wings*]

Gésiers Confits

GIZZARDS CONFIT

Confit gizzards from ducks can be used in many dishes. They flavor soups, salads, stews, and bean dishes. *Confit* gizzards lose their rubbery and chewy texture and become tender, yet resilient. Gizzards from moulard ducks are larger than those from a regular duck. For example, one moulard gizzard is enough to garnish an individual salad; two or three are needed from a Pekin duck. Moulard duck gizzards can be purchased in 1-pound bags (see Shopping Sources, page 189). Otherwise, you can freeze the duck gizzards until you have enough to make a *confit*.

1½ tablespoons coarse salt
1 teaspoon freshly ground black
  pepper
1 teaspoon quatre épices (see
  recipe page 175)
1 teaspoon thyme
1½ teaspoons crushed rosemary
½ bay leaf, crushed

6 cloves
1 head garlic, peeled
1 pound moulard duck gizzards
  or Pekin duck gizzards
3 cups rendered duck fat (see
  recipe page 176)
Vegetable oil, optional

At least a week before you plan to use the gizzards, combine the salt, pepper, *quatre épices,* thyme, rosemary, and bay leaf in a mixing bowl. Pierce the garlic with the cloves and add them to the bowl. Stir in the gizzards, cover, and refrigerate overnight.

The next day, remove the gizzards from the refrigerator and wipe off the herbs and salt. Reserve the garlic and cloves. Heat the duck fat in a heavy casserole, such as an enamel cast-iron pot.

When the fat is just warm, add the gizzards to the pot along with the garlic and cloves, and cook, uncovered, for 1½ hours for the moulard duck gizzards or 1 hour for the Pekin duck gizzards—or until the gizzards are very tender. Remove the gizzards from the pot and pass the fat through a very fine sieve. It would be more practical to store the gizzards in small glass jars or heavy crocks since they can be used in small quantities in many dishes. Fill the containers with boiling water, pour it out, and let dry. Place the gizzards in the containers and pour the hot fat over them. They should be completely covered by the fat. Cool at room temperature, then cover and refrigerate.

If you plan to store the *confit* for an extended time, cover the solid fat with a $\frac{1}{2}$-inch layer of vegetable oil to form an airtight seal. Refrigerate for at least one week before eating; it can keep up to three months. [*Yield: 1 pound*]

La Cuisse de Dinde Confite

TURKEY LEG CONFIT

Turkey has leaner meat than duck and carries little fat. For this reason duck fat is used when making turkey *confit*. Turkey *confit* can be served in the same way as duck *confit*: sautéed, added to salads and soups, or combined with foie gras in a terrine.

4 whole turkey legs, about 1 pound each
4½ tablespoons coarse salt
1 teaspoon freshly ground black pepper
2 teaspoons thyme

1 head garlic, peeled
4 cloves
2 quarts rendered duck fat (see recipe 176)
Vegetable oil, optional

At least a week before serving, rinse and dry the turkey legs. Place them in a large mixing bowl. Combine the coarse salt, pepper, and thyme. Rub the mixture over the legs. Pierce the garlic with the cloves and add them to the turkey. Cover and refrigerate for 36 hours. When ready to cook the legs, melt the fat in a large heavy pot—enamel-coated cast-iron works particularly well. Meanwhile, wipe the salt mixture off the legs. Reserve the garlic and cloves. When the fat is melted but not hot, add the turkey to the pot along with the garlic and cloves. Cook over low heat for 3 hours, or until the meat can be pierced easily with a straw or toothpick. Remove the legs from the pot and pass the cooking fat through a fine sieve.

To store the legs, use glass jars or heavy crocks with wide openings. Fill the containers with boiling water, pour it out, and let dry. Arrange the legs in them, pour the hot fat over the turkey to cover completely, and let cool to room temperature. Cover and refrigerate.

If you plan to store the *confit* for an extended time, cover the solid fat with a ½-inch layer of vegetable oil to form an airtight seal. Refrigerate for at least one week before eating; it can keep up to three months.

Remove the containers from the refrigerator a few hours before cooking to soften the fat. Remove the turkey pieces from the fat. The legs may be prepared in two different ways: either steamed on top of a *couscoussier* or a steamer for 10 minutes, or roasted in the oven. If you choose to roast them, place them in a 300 degree oven for 10 minutes, turn up the heat to 400 degrees, and roast until golden brown, about 5 minutes.   [*Yield: 8 servings*]

Confit de Porc

PORK LOIN CONFIT

Pork becomes very succulent when made into *confit*. It is an essential ingredient in *garbure*, a cabbage soup (see recipe page 79), and is also delicious when cooked with lentils and other beans.

1 2-pound boned pork loin
4 tablespoons coarse salt
1 teaspoon freshly ground black
   pepper
½ teaspoon quatre épices (see
   recipe page 175)

1 teaspoon thyme
1 garlic head, peeled
4 cloves
6 cups rendered pork fat
Vegetable oil, optional

At least one week before you plan to serve it, combine the salt, pepper, *quatre épices,* and thyme in a mixing bowl. Place the loin in the bowl and rub it with the mixture. Pierce the garlic with the cloves and add them to the bowl. Cover and refrigerate overnight.

Remove the pork loin from the refrigerator and wipe off the salt and spices. Reserve the garlic and cloves. Heat the pork fat in a heavy casserole such as an enamel-coated cast-iron pot. When the fat is warm, add the loin along with the garlic and the cloves. Cook very slowly for 2 hours, or until the meat can be easily pierced with a straw or a toothpick. Remove the meat from the pot and pass the cooking fat through a fine sieve.

Fill a heavy crock large enough to hold the meat with boiling water, pour it out, and let dry. Place the loin in it and pour the hot fat over it. The meat should be completely covered by the fat. Cool to room temperature. Cover and refrigerate.

If you plan to store the *confit* for an extended time, cover the solid fat with a ½-inch layer of vegetable oil to form an airtight seal. Keep in the refrigerator for at least a week before using and up to three months.   [*Yield: 8 servings*]

Cuisse de Canard Confite dans le Bouillon

DUCK LEG CONFIT IN BROTH

This is a simple but tasty dish that is a twist on a *pot-au-feu*. If you happen to have some leftover duck consommé, use it for the broth. Otherwise, use a duck stock (see page 173).

2 ½ quarts consommé or duck stock
½ cup dry Madeira wine
Salt and freshly ground black pepper to taste (optional)
2 large carrots, each cut into 12 sticks

6 small turnips, peeled
1 small bulb celeriac, cut into 12 sticks
12 small potatoes, peeled
6 duck legs confit, fat removed (see page 46)

Combine the stock and the Madeira in a large saucepan and bring to a boil.

Lightly season with salt and pepper, if desired. Add the vegetables to the broth, cook them until soft, then remove. The turnips will be done first, in about 5 minutes; the potatoes last, taking about 10 minutes. Place them on a warm serving platter with a little broth and keep warm until ready to serve. Heat the duck legs in the simmering broth for 10 minutes, or until they are heated through. Add the legs to the serving platter. Distribute the meat and vegetables, along with some broth, among six soup bowls. Serve with cornichons on the side.   [*Yield: 6 servings*]

Gésiers Confits au Zinfandel

GIZZARDS CONFIT IN ZINFANDEL

In Gascon cooking, gizzards are often used in garnishes, but they can also be served on their own. This recipe can be served as an appetizer or, as an entrée when a simple meal is desired. It goes well with noodles or rice pilaf.

1 tablespoon duck fat from the
  confit
½ carrot, minced
½ turnip, minced
2 shallots, minced
2 cups Zinfandel wine, or
  another good robust red wine

12 gizzards confit (see page 48)
2 tablespoons unsalted butter, cut
  into small cubes
Salt and freshly ground black
  pepper to taste

Heat the duck fat in a small saucepan over medium heat and sauté the carrot, turnip, and shallots for 8 to 10 minutes, or until they are soft. Add the wine and simmer for 15 minutes, or until reduced by half.

Remove the gizzards from their fat and wipe off the excess. Cut the gizzards into thin slices.

Degrease and strain the sauce through a fine sieve and return it to the saucepan. Add the gizzard slices and simmer for 5 minutes to heat them through. Whisk in the butter, a few pieces at a time, until well incorporated. Season with salt and pepper, and serve immediately.   [*Yield: 6 servings*]

Ailerons et Gésiers
de Canard Confit aux Lentilles

WINGS AND GIZZARDS CONFIT WITH LENTILS

1 pound lentils
5 tablespoons duck fat from the
  confit
2 onions, minced
3 garlic cloves, minced
2 teaspoons tomato paste
1 cup white wine

6 moulard or 12 Pekin duck
  wings confit (see page 46)
6 gizzards confit (see page 48)
½ pound lean pork sausage
Salt and freshly ground black
  pepper to taste

Rinse the lentils thoroughly, removing any stones or dirt. In a large pot, heat 3 tablespoons of the duck fat over a high flame.

Add the onions, garlic, and tomato paste, and sauté until golden brown, stirring often. Stir in the lentils and the wine. Cover with water and season with salt and pepper. Bring to a boil, cover, and cook over medium heat for 30 minutes, or until the lentils are soft. Add water to the pot if necessary.

Meanwhile, wipe off the fat from the duck wings and remove the meat from the bones. Wipe off the fat from the gizzards and cut them into thin slices.

Heat 2 tablespoons of the duck fat in a frying pan and sauté the sausage until golden on all sides. Remove from the pan and cut into ½-inch slices.

Preheat the oven to 350 degrees.

In a large casserole dish, layer the wing meat and the gizzard slices. Spoon the lentils on top and garnish with the sausage. Bake for 15 minutes and serve immediately.   [*Yield: 6 servings*]

Cuisse de Canard aux Pommes Sautées dans Sa Graisse Salée

DUCK CONFIT WITH SAUTÉED POTATOES IN DUCK FAT

This is the most traditional way to eat duck or goose legs *confit*. Usually the legs are slowly sautéed in their fat to crisp the skin while leaving the meat moist and savory. Here they are first heated in a steamer to eliminate some of the saltiness and fat. The legs are then put under the broiler for a few minutes just to crisp the skin. The potatoes are cooked in the fat from the preserved duck. Sometimes minced garlic and parsley are sprinkled over the potatoes toward the end of the cooking.

6 duck legs confit (see page 46)
6 medium potatoes, peeled
¼ cup duck fat from the confit
Salt and freshly ground black
*   pepper to taste*

2 garlic cloves, minced (optional)
3 tablespoons minced parsley
*   (optional)*

Remove the duck legs from the fat and wipe off the excess. Set aside.

Bring a large quantity of water to a boil in the bottom part of a *couscoussiér* or a steamer. Arrange the legs in the top part, cover, and steam for 10 minutes.

Cut the potatoes into ¼-inch-thick slices.

Heat the duck fat in a large heavy skillet over high heat. When it starts to smoke, add the potatoes. Turn them quickly to coat them with the fat and brown them slightly. Lower the heat, cover, and cook for 30 minutes, or until the potatoes are soft, shaking the pan occasionally.

Preheat the broiler.

Place the legs on a baking sheet, skin side up, and place them under the broiler for 3 to 5 minutes, or until the skin is crisp and golden brown.

Meanwhile, remove the cover from the skillet, turn up the heat to high, add the garlic and parsley, if desired, and sauté the potatoes until crisp and brown. Sprinkle with salt and pepper.

Arrange the duck legs and the potatoes on a serving platter and serve immediately.   [*Yield: 6 servings*]

MAGRET

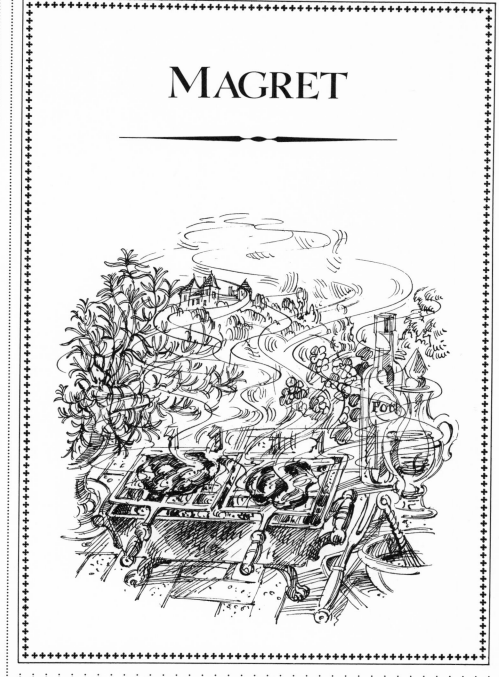

*A*bout twenty-five years ago, the idea came to me to serve the red meat from the breasts of foie gras ducks as if they were beef. Until then, these meaty, oversized duck breasts were always cooked *confit-*style, that is, in their own fat. I knew it would be a challenge to get people to accept such a radical change, so a little artifice was necessary at first. In the beginning I removed all the skin and fat so the duck breast would resemble some sort of red meat. The *magret* was then pan-sautéed like a steak and served with various sauces. The first customers who sampled it indeed thought they were eating steak. When I let them in on the secret, they were astounded.

Today, of course, *magret* is widely enjoyed in France in many forms— even as carpaccio.

In France, the term *magret* is clearly defined as the breast of a fattened moulard duck, while everything else is simply duck breast. In the United States the term was tossed around carelessly for several years until 1986, when the SDA issued a regulation based on the French term. Now in this country, *magret* should be used only to define moulard duck breast.

Magret is a bit chewier (this is particuliary true in the United States) than regular duck breast, because the pectoral muscles of fattened birds become stronger as the liver enlarges. What is lost in tenderness, however, is gained in flavor—the liver imparts, to the meat, a richness absent in regular duck breast. *Magret* is most tender when sliced thinly on the diagonal just before serving.

The recipes in this book that call for *magret* can be adapted to regular duck breast; simply reduce the cooking time slightly, as suggested in each recipe. Keep in mind that one side of a whole *magret,* or a single steak, may weigh up to one pound and can serve two people, depending on the preparation. When the term *magret* is used in the recipes that follow, it means one of these steaks, not the duck's entire breast. In the recipes in this book, two *magrets* serve three to four people. Also, cooking times for the following recipes are for rare to medium-rare, which is the best way to serve *magret.*

Le Magret Pelé Sauté à l'Échalote

SAUTÉED MAGRET WITH SHALLOTS

This recipe is adapted from the well-known dish from the southwest of France, *entrecôte bordelaise*.

4 magrets (2 whole breasts),
   about 1 pound each
$\frac{1}{3}$ cup rendered duck fat, at room
   temperature (see recipe page
   176)
3 garlic cloves, thinly sliced

1 teaspoon thyme
Salt and freshly ground black
   pepper to taste
4 shallots, finely chopped
6 tablespoons cold unsalted butter
   ($\frac{3}{4}$ stick), cut into small cubes

Remove the skin from the *magrets* and reserve it to make rendered duck fat (see page 176).

Lightly pound the meat to flatten it and rub both sides with the duck fat, garlic, and thyme. Marinate the meat at room temperature for 2 hours.

Remove the *magret* from the fat and remove and discard the garlic slices clinging to it. Season with salt and pepper.

Heat a large heavy pan over high flame and sauté the *magrets* until medium-rare, about 5 to 6 minutes on each side. Remove the meat from the pan and keep it warm while making the sauce.

Add the shallots to the pan and sauté them over medium heat for about 4 minutes. Stir the butter pieces, a few at a time, into the pan. Remove the pan from the heat. Cut the *magrets* diagonally into thin slices and arrange on warmed dinner plates. Stir the juices from the *magret* into the sauce, then spoon the sauce over the meat. Serve immediately with french fries.　[*Yield: 6 to 8 servings*]

NOTE: If using Pekin duck breasts, serve one breast per person and adjust the cooking time to 3 to 4 minutes on each side.

Magret Grillé sans Sa Peau

GRILLED MAGRET

4 magrets (2 whole breasts),
about 1 pound each
Coarse salt and freshly ground
black pepper to taste
2 teaspoons rosemary
1 teaspoon thyme

½ cup rendered duck fat, at room
temperature (see recipe page
176)
4 garlic cloves, thinly sliced
Auscitaine sauce, optional (see
recipe page 158)

Remove the skin from the magret and reserve it to make rendered duck fat (see page 176).

Lightly pound the meat to flatten it and rub both sides with the coarse salt, pepper, rosemary, and thyme. Place the *magrets* in a shallow dish and coat them with the duck fat. Add the garlic to the dish and marinate for at least 2 hours at room temperature.

Light a charcoal fire and allow the coals to become red hot. Remove the *magret* from the fat and discard any garlic clinging to it.

Grill the meat over hot coals for 5 to 6 minutes on each side and let stand in a warm place for 10 minutes before serving. Cut the *magret* diagonally into thin slices and arrange on warmed dinner plates. Pour some of the juices from the *magret* over the meat, season with coarse salt and pepper to taste, and serve immediately with the Auscitaine sauce if desired. [*Yield: 6 to 8 servings*]

NOTE: If using Pekin duck breasts, serve one breast per person and adjust the cooking time to 4 to 5 minutes on each side.

Sports

Now that the days of musketeering are long gone, Gascons have devised other sports to keep themselves amused. The English have had an unusually strong influence on the Gascon taste for leisure activities. Although British sovereignty ended a long time ago, they found Gascony to their liking and returned in peacetime to commandeer the area as their vacationland of choice. With them, they brought their own diversions: The first golf course on the continent was built on Gascon soil for the holidaymakers' amusement. And to this day, for a reason inexplicable even to the natives, in Gascony, rugby (not soccer as in the rest of France) is the football game of choice.

Of course in addition to these "imports" the Gascons have some sports of their own devising. The two most popular are the game of *pétanque*—found throughout southern Europe—and *pelote Basque*, a Basque invention related to jai alai.

Pétanque is played by propelling a steel ball through the air along the ground toward another, smaller ball called the jack or *cochonnet*. *Pétanque* is played on a gritty or stony strip, usually found in the central square of the village.

Pelote Basque is named for the hard rubber-cored ball—*pelota*—covered with a layer of linen thread and two layers of goat skin. The game is played in a four-walled court, by two players or teams of players. The object is to hit the ball against the front wall (*fronton*) so that the opponents will be unable to return it and will lose a point. In the hands of a master, the *pelota* has been clocked at 150 miles per hour.

Magret de Canard dans Sa Peau au Gros Sel

BROILED MAGRET

4 magrets (2 whole breasts),
    about 1 pound each
¼ cup vegetable oil

Coarse salt and crushed white
    pepper to taste

Preheat the broiler.

Using a sharp knife, make four incisions in the skin of each duck breast in a crisscross pattern. The cuts should be deep, but should not go all the way through the skin. This will help the fat melt while cooking. Rub the *magrets* on both sides with the oil and sprinkle with the coarse salt and pepper.

Heat a large frying pan over high heat and cook the *magrets,* skin side up, for 8 to 10 minutes. Transfer the meat to a baking sheet, skin side up, and place under the broiler for 2 or 3 minutes, until the skin is crisp and golden brown. (The meat should be cooked closer to medium than rare, otherwise the fat will not melt enough.) Cut the *magrets* diagonally into thin slices and arrange on warmed dinner plates. Serve with potatoes sautéed in duck fat.
[*Yield: 6 to 8 servings*]

NOTE: If using Pekin duck breasts, serve one breast per person and adjust the cooking time to 5 to 6 minutes in the sauté pan and 2 to 3 minutes under the broiler.

Magret aux Fruits Frais

MAGRET SAUTÉED WITH FRESH FRUIT

This palate-teasing recipe dates back to the Middle Ages.

1 pound fresh berries (raspberries,
  boysenberries, black currants,
  blackberries, wild strawberries,
  or any combination)
¾ cup port wine
⅓ cup Armagnac

4 magrets (2 whole breasts),
  about 1 pound each
Salt and freshly ground black
  pepper to taste
3 tablespoons vegetable oil
½ cup water

In a heavy saucepan combine ¾ pound of the berries, the port wine, and the Armagnac. Bring to a boil and simmer for 15 minutes, or until the mixture is reduced by half and is thick and lightly caramelized. Pass the sauce through a fine sieve to remove the seeds and reserve until ready to use.

Remove the skin from the duck breasts and reserve it to make rendered duck fat (see page 176). Season the meat with salt and pepper. In a large frying pan, heat the oil over high heat and sauté the duck breasts for 4 to 5 minutes on each side. Remove the meat from the pan and keep warm.

Discard the fat from the pan and deglaze with water. Stir the prepared fruit purée into the pan and reduce by half. Add the remaining ¼ pound berries to the sauce and cook briefly, just to warm. Cut the *magrets* diagonally into thin slices and arrange on warmed serving plates. Stir the juice from the meat into the sauce and spoon it over the breasts. Serve immediately.   [*Yield: 6 to 8 servings*]

NOTE: If using Pekin duck breasts, serve one breast per person and adjust the cooking time to 3 to 4 minutes on each side.

Magret "en Chevreuil"

MAGRET GAME-STYLE

The traditional game marinade works well with red duck meat.

4 magrets (2 whole breasts),
   about 1 pound each
3 garlic cloves, crushed
1 bay leaf
2 teaspoons thyme
10 black peppercorns
2 cloves
⅓ cup Armagnac

1 ½ cups red wine
¼ cup red wine vinegar
¼ cup vegetable oil
2 shallots, finely chopped
1 teaspoon tomato paste
2 tablespoons heavy cream
Salt and freshly ground black
   pepper to taste

The day before serving the duck breasts, remove the skin from the *magrets* and reserve it to make rendered duck fat (see page 176). Combine the garlic cloves, bay leaf, thyme, peppercorns, cloves, Armagnac, red wine, and vinegar in a shallow dish. Add the *magrets* to the dish and coat them well with the marinade. Refrigerate for at least 12 hours.

A few hours before cooking, remove the duck from the refrigerator to bring the meat to room temperature. Remove the *magrets* from the marinade and dry them with paper towels. Strain the marinade and reserve the liquid.

Heat 2 tablespoons of the oil in a large frying pan over a high flame, and sauté half of the duck for 4 minutes on each side. Set them aside in a warm place. Add the remaining oil and sauté the remaining duck for 4 minutes on each side. Remove them from the pan and keep warm.

Pour off the fat from the pan, add the shallots and the tomato paste, stir well, and cook over medium heat for 2 minutes. Deglaze with the reserved marinade and reduce by half. Pass the sauce through a fine sieve, then return it to the pan. Bring to a boil and add the cream. Cook for 30 seconds. Season the sauce with salt and pepper to taste. To serve, slice the *magrets* diagonally into thin slices and arrange on warmed dinner plates. Spoon the sauce over the meat and serve.   [*Yield: 6 to 8 servings*]

NOTE: If using Pekin duck breasts, use one breast per person and adjust the cooking time to 3 minutes on each side.

Le Magret au Pot

7 cups duck stock (see page 173)
¼ cup dry Madeira wine
Salt and freshly ground black
    pepper to taste
4 magrets (2 whole breasts),
    about 1 pound each
6 medium carrots, halved
    crosswise

6 small turnips
12 small leeks, green and white
    part
Coarse salt
Sharp mustard as a condiment

In a large saucepan, combine the duck stock and the Madeira. Bring to a boil and simmer for 15 minutes. Season with salt and pepper to taste.

Meanwhile, trim the *magrets* and slice off about three fourths of the fat from the skin. About ⅛ inch of fat should be left on each *magret*. Season the meat lightly with salt and heavily with pepper.

When the stock is boiling, add the vegetables to the pan. The turnips should be cooked first, in about 7 to 8 minutes, the carrots and the leeks in 12 to 15 minutes. As each vegetable is cooked, remove with a slotted spoon and keep warm.

Bring the stock back to a low simmer, add the *magrets* to the pan, and poach for 9 minutes. Remove the meat from the pan, cut it diagonally into thin slices, and place on a warm serving platter. Arrange the vegetables on the platter and serve the broth on the side.

Serve each person a soup bowl of meat, vegetables, and broth. Use coarse salt and sharp mustard as condiments. [*Yield: 6 to 8 servings*]

NOTE: If using Pekin duck breasts, serve one breast per person and adjust the cooking time to 4 minutes.

Magret Chaud Fumé

WARMED SMOKED MAGRET

This dish is particularly appealing if you happen to own a home smoker, but it is also excellent prepared with unsmoked *magret*. The mushrooms in the vinaigrette are used as a binder. The vinaigrette will remain emulsified when poured over the warm breasts. This trick can be applied to any warm salad.

$\frac{1}{4}$ *cup red wine*
7 tablespoons red wine vinegar
1 $\frac{1}{3}$ cups olive oil
Salt and freshly ground black
  pepper to taste
4 large white mushrooms,
  stemmed and chopped

1 pound celeriac
4 magrets (2 whole breasts),
  about 1 pound each
2 tablespoons vegetable oil
Truffle juice to taste (optional)

In a mixing bowl combine the wine, wine vinegar, olive oil, salt, and pepper. Pour the mixture into the bowl of a food processor or blender and add the mushrooms. Purée quickly into a smooth mixture. Set aside.

Cut the celeriac into $\frac{1}{2}$-inch-thick slices and cook in lightly salted water for 8 minutes, or until tender. Drain and keep warm until ready to use.

Remove the skin from the *magrets* and season them with salt and pepper. Heat the vegetable oil in a large frying pan over high heat and sauté the *magrets* 4 to 5 minutes on each side. Remove them from the pan, and, if desired, smoke the meat for 2 minutes. Otherwise, let the meat rest for 5 minutes in a warm place.

Spoon some of the vinaigrette on each serving plate. Cut the *magrets* diagonally into thin slices and arrange on top of the sauce. Combine the juices from the *magret* with the truffle juice (optional) and spoon it over the meat. Garnish with the celeriac and serve immediately.   [*Yield: 6 to 8 servings*]

NOTE: If using Pekin duck breasts, serve one breast per person and adjust the cooking time to 3 to 4 minutes on each side.

Magret

SOUPS

La Crème de Haricots

CREAM OF FRESH BEAN SOUP

This soup should be made only with fresh white beans. Traditionally, diners mix a little red wine into their plates when the soup is almost finished, then drink it. According to Gascon custom, this practice, called *chabrot au vin rouge,* guarantees good digestion.

FOR THE SOUP:

2 tablespoons rendered duck fat
(see recipe page 176)
2 ounces prosciutto, minced
2 carrots, minced
1 turnip, minced
6 celery stalks
1 garlic head, peeled and minced
2 onions, peeled

2 cloves
2 pounds fresh white beans,
shelled
2 quarts warm water
1 bay leaf
$\frac{1}{2}$ teaspoon thyme
Salt and freshly ground black
pepper to taste

FOR THE OMELET:

$\frac{1}{2}$ cup fresh bread crumbs
$\frac{1}{4}$ cup milk
3 eggs
4 ounces sweet bulk sausage
2 garlic cloves, minced
2 tablespoons minced parsley

3 tablespoons heavy cream
Salt and freshly ground black
pepper
1 tablespoon rendered duck fat
(see recipe page 176)

Heat the duck fat in a large pot and sauté the ham, carrots, turnip, celery, and garlic over medium-high heat for 10 minutes, or until golden. Pierce the onions with the cloves and add to the pot along with the beans. Stir well. Add the warm water, bay leaf, thyme, salt, and pepper. Bring to a boil, then lower to a simmer. Cook, covered, for $1\frac{1}{2}$ hours, or until the beans are very soft.

Meanwhile, soak the bread crumbs in the milk for 10 minutes. Drain and squeeze out as much liquid as possible. Beat the eggs in a mixing bowl, stir in the sausage meat, soaked bread crumbs, garlic, parsley, and cream. Season with salt and pepper. Heat the duck fat in a small frying pan, pour the egg mixture in it and cook over medium-low heat until the eggs are set, about

10 minutes. Turn the omelet over and cook for another 10 minutes. Set aside until ready to use.

When the beans are cooked, remove and discard the onions with the cloves and the bay leaf. Purée the remaining soup in a food processor until smooth. Return the soup to the pot, gently slide the omelet into it, and simmer for another 30 minutes. Season to taste with salt and pepper.

To serve, remove the omelet from the pot and slice like a tart. Place a piece of the omelet on each soup plate and ladle some of the soup over it.   [*Yield: 6 servings*]

Soupe de Lentilles

LENTIL SOUP

1 pound lentils
2 tablespoons rendered duck fat
  (see recipe page 176)
$\frac{1}{4}$ pound prosciutto, cut into
  small cubes
36 small pearl onions, peeled
1 tablespoon tomato paste

2 quarts water
$\frac{1}{2}$ cup heavy cream
Salt and freshly ground black
  pepper to taste
$\frac{1}{4}$ pound slab bacon, cut into
  small cubes

Preheat the oven to 350 degrees.

Pick any stones or dirt from the lentils then rinse the lentils thoroughly. Drain well.

Heat the duck fat in a large, ovenproof pot over medium heat. Add the prosciutto and the onions, and cook for 10 to 15 minutes, until the onions are lightly golden. Stir in the tomato paste and the lentils. Add the water to the pot, bring to a boil, cover, and cook in the oven for 30 to 40 minutes, or until the lentils are very soft.

When the lentils are cooked, add the cream to the pot, season to taste with salt and pepper, and bring to a boil on top of the stove. Cook for 10 minutes. Pour the soup into the bowl of a food processor or blender and purée to a coarse consistency. Sauté the bacon in a small frying pan over medium-high heat until golden and crisp. Drain on paper towel.

Reheat the soup briefly, adjust the seasoning, and pour into a soup terrine. Sprinkle the bacon on top and serve immediately.   [*Yield: 6 servings*]

Bouillon de Dinde à la Dinde Fumée

TURKEY BROTH WITH SMOKED TURKEY

2 turkey carcasses or 2 whole legs
8 celery stalks, coarsely chopped
1 carrot, coarsely chopped
1 turnip, coarsely chopped
1 large garlic head, peeled
1 onion, peeled

6 cloves
4 quarts water
$\frac{1}{2}$ cup Armagnac
Salt and freshly ground black
    pepper to taste

GARNISH:

2 ounces smoked turkey breast or
    smoked magret
1 small leek, white part only

$\frac{1}{2}$ carrot
2 tablespoons rendered duck fat
  (see recipe page 176)

Place the turkey carcasses or legs, celery, carrot, turnip, and garlic in a large pot. Pierce the onion with four cloves and add it to the pot. Cover with the water and bring to a boil. Boil for 15 minutes, skimming often. Reduce the heat to a low simmer and cook undisturbed for 6 hours, skimming occasionally.

Carefully remove the meat and vegetables from the pot and pass the broth through a fine sieve lined with a clean linen cloth. You should have 2 $\frac{1}{2}$ quarts of broth; add some water if necessary. Pour the broth into a large saucepan and add the remaining cloves and the Armagnac. Season with salt and pepper. Bring the soup to a simmer and reduce for 15 minutes.

Meanwhile, cut the smoked turkey into $\frac{1}{8}$-inch strips. Cut the leek and carrot into a very fine julienne. Heat the duck fat over medium-high heat in a small frying pan. Add the julienned carrot and leek, and sauté until golden and soft. Remove the vegetables from the pan with a slotted spoon and drain briefly on paper towels.

Taste the broth and adjust the seasoning, remove the cloves, and pour into a soup terrine. Garnish with the sautéed vegetables and the smoked turkey. Serve immediately.   [*Yield: 6 servings*]

Soupe de Poule aux Trois Omelettes

CHICKEN SOUP WITH THREE OMELETS

In Gascony, small fat omelets, called *farci*, are often added to soups. It is an inexpensive way to enrich them, as well as add flavor and texture. In this case, the omelets not only give flavor to the broth but also clarify it.

This recipe makes a nice cold-weather brunch dish.

THE SOUP:

1 stewing hen or capon, about 5 pounds
3 onions, peeled
1 celery stalk
2 garlic cloves, peeled

1 large shallot, peeled
4 leeks, cleaned and trimmed
3 turnips, peeled
Salt and freshly ground black pepper to taste

THE OMELETS:

12 eggs
¾ cup fresh bread crumbs
Salt and freshly ground black pepper to taste
6 teaspoons rendered duck fat (see recipe page 176)

3 garlic cloves, minced
1 tablespoon chopped parsley
1 onion, minced
1 medium tomato, peeled, seeded, and chopped
1 teaspoon tomato paste

Blanch the hen in a large pot of boiling water for 5 minutes. Drain, then return the hen to the pot along with all the vegetables. Cover with water and bring to a boil. Let boil for 15 minutes, skimming often. Reduce the heat to a low simmer and cook for 4 hours, skimming occasionally.

Remove the hen and the vegetables from the pot and pass the broth through a fine sieve. Return the broth to the pot. You should have about 3 quarts; if not, reduce the broth. Season with salt and pepper.

To make the omelets: Divide the eggs among three small mixing bowls. Add ¼ cup bread crumbs to each and season with salt and pepper.

Heat 2 teaspoons of the duck fat in a 6-inch frying pan. Add the garlic and cook over medium heat for 5 minutes, do not burn the garlic or it will develop a bitter taste. Meanwhile, add the parsley to one of the mixing bowls. Pour the mixture into the frying pan and cook until the omelet is set, about 3 minutes on each side. Remove from the pan and set aside.

Heat 2 teaspoons of the duck fat in the frying pan. Add the onion and cook over medium-high heat until soft and golden, about 8 minutes. Pour one of the remaining egg mixtures over the onion and cook until the omelet is set, about 3 minutes on each side. Remove from the pan and set aside.

Heat the remaining duck fat in the frying pan and cook the tomato over low heat until all the liquid has evaporated, about 10 minutes. Stir the tomato paste into the remaining egg mixture and pour it into the frying pan. Cook until the omelet is set, about 3 minutes on each side. Remove from the pan and set aside.

Gently slide the omelets into the chicken broth and simmer for 15 minutes. To serve, place a piece of each omelet along with some hot broth into warmed soup bowls. [*Yield: 12 servings*]

Bouillon Clair de Faisan au Foie Gras

CLEAR PHEASANT BROTH WITH FOIE GRAS

2 onions, peeled
3 pheasant carcasses
1 chicken carcass
1 leek, trimmed
2 carrots, peeled
1 turnip, peeled
6 celery stalks
10 black peppercorns

Salt to taste
$\frac{1}{4}$ cup Madeira wine
$\frac{1}{8}$ teaspoon saffron
1 small lobe of a fresh foie gras,
    about 8 ounces
Coarse salt to taste
Crushed white peppercorns to
    taste

Preheat the broiler.

Cut the onions in half crosswise and place under the broiler cut side up. Grill until the onions are very dark, almost burned.

Place the pheasant and chicken carcasses in a large pot, cover with cold water, bring to a boil, and drain immediately. Return the carcasses to the pot along with the vegetables and the peppercorns. Cover with cold water and bring to a low simmer. Cook undisturbed for 6 hours, skimming once in a while and making sure the broth simmers slowly. The broth will remain clear if cooked over low heat and the liquid is not stirred.

Remove the carcasses and the vegetables, and pass the broth through a fine sieve lined with a clean linen towel. You should have 2 quarts of broth. If not, reduce over low heat.

Pour the broth into a smaller pot, season with salt, and add the Madeira and the saffron. Bring to a very slow boil and simmer, partially covered, for 1 hour.

When ready to serve, cut the foie gras into $\frac{1}{4}$-inch cubes and roll in a mixture of coarse salt and crushed white pepper. Divide the foie gras cubes among six soup bowls and pour the hot broth over them. Serve immediately. [*Yield: 6 servings*]

Le Bouillon de Queue de Boeuf au Fenouil

OXTAIL SOUP WITH FENNEL

3 ¾ to 4 pounds oxtails
¼ pound fresh pork rind
3 tablespoons coarse salt
6 cloves
3 onions, peeled

6 carrots, coarsely chopped
3 turnips, coarsely chopped
5 celery stalks, coarsely chopped
3 fennel bulbs
1 calf's foot

THE MAYONNAISE:

1 egg yolk
1 teaspoon mustard
½ cup vegetable oil

Salt and freshly ground black
  pepper to taste
¼ cup good-quality olive oil

The day before serving the soup, remove most of the fat from the oxtail. In a large mixing bowl, rub the oxtail and the pork rind with the coarse salt. Cover and let stand overnight in the refrigerator.

The next day, wipe off the salt, place the meat in a stockpot, and cover with cold water. Add the cloves and bring to a boil. Drain and rinse the meat under cold running water.

Preheat the broiler.

Halve the onions crosswise and grill under the broiler on both sides until they are dark.

Put the carrots, turnips, onions, celery, and two fennel bulbs in the bottom of a large soup pot. Add the oxtail, the pork rind, and the calf's foot, and cover with cold water. Bring to a boil and skim off the fat. Lower the flame and simmer for 6 hours, skimming occasionally.

Meanwhile, combine the yolk, mustard, salt, and pepper in a small mixing bowl. Stir in the oils, whisking constantly, in a slow steady stream to form an emulsion. Whisk until the oils are incorporated and the mixture is thick and firm. Set aside until ready to use.

Cut the remaining fennel into very thin strips.

Remove the meats from the pot and reserve them for possible later use, such as in oxtail salad. Discard the calf's foot, pork rind, and vegetables.

Pass the stock through a fine sieve, return to the pot, and heat it.

To serve, spoon some of the mayonnaise into the bottom of each soup bowl, add some fennel strips, and ladle the stock over it. Serve immediately. [Yield: 6 servings]

La Garbure

GARBURE

Originally *garbure,* the classic stew-like soup from Gascony, was a simple cabbage-and-fresh-bacon soup that farmers cooked all day in a corner of their fireplace. The soup was always cooking, day after day, waiting for the workers to come back from the fields. Once in a while, the farmer would regarnish the pot by throwing in a handful of fresh vegetables picked from his garden, or maybe a few potatoes. A flat omelet or *farci,* made of bread crumbs, garlic, chicken gizzards, liver, and heart, was often added to make the soup a more substantial meal. The vegetables changed depending on the season: cabbage in winter, carrots and turnips in the spring, fava beans in June, young peas and fresh beans in July. Dried beans, chestnuts, or potatoes could be added as well to enrich the soup.

The meats, added to the soup, depend on whether it is to be served as a simple family dinner or for a more elaborate gala. *Confit-*style duck or goose legs, gizzards, necks, or various cuts of pork are the best choices.

This version is served at the Hôtel de France. The cabbage is lightly "fried" in duck fat before being added to the soup. It gives the soup a slightly caramelized flavor.

*3 pounds duck or chicken
 carcasses and wing tips*
4 turnips, peeled
4 leeks, white and green parts
3 onions, peeled
6 carrots, peeled
6 celery stalks, chopped
12 garlic cloves, peeled
½ pound fresh pork rind
6 eggs
¼ cup chopped parsley
1 pound sausage meat

*¾ cup rendered duck fat (see
 recipe page 176)*
1 pork loin confit *(see page 51)*
2 duck legs confit *(see page 46)*
2 heads savoy cabbage
*Salt and freshly ground black
 pepper to taste*
4 gizzards confit, *thinly sliced
 (see page 48)*
12 garlic cloves confit *(see page
 177)*

The day before serving the *garbure,* place the carcasses, wing tips, turnips, leeks, two onions, two carrots, and four celery stalks in a large stockpot, cover with cold water, and bring to a boil over high heat. Lower the flame

to a bare simmer and cook, skimming occasionally, for 3 to 4 hours. Pass the stock through a fine sieve and refrigerate until ready to use.

The next day, coarsely chop the remaining onion, celery stalks, and six garlic cloves. Heat 2 tablespoons of the duck fat in a large pot and sauté the chopped vegetables, and the pork rind for 5 minutes. Add the cold stock and bring it to a slow boil. Meanwhile, mince six garlic cloves and combine with the eggs, the parsley, and the sausage meat.

Heat 2 tablespoons of the duck fat in a large frying pan, pour in the egg mixture and cook over medium heat for 10 minutes on each side, or until the omelet is completely set and golden brown on both sides. Gently slide the omelet into the stock. Add the pork loin and the duck legs and cook for 30 minutes. The soup should simmer, not boil.

Cut the remaining carrots into 1-inch chunks.

Cut the cabbage into quarters and blanch in salted boiling water for 5 minutes. Drain well. Heat the remaining duck fat in a small saucepan to the smoking point. Place the cabbage on a baking sheet and ladle the hot fat over it. Be careful as it will sizzle. Add the fried cabbage and the carrots to the pot and cook for 30 to 40 minutes. Taste and adjust the seasoning with salt and pepper.

Ten minutes before serving, add the sliced gizzards and garlic *confit* to the pot and simmer. To serve, ladle some of the meat and vegetables into serving soup plates and pour some hot broth over them. [*Yield: 12 servings*]

Soupe à la Citrouille

PUMPKIN SOUP

3 tablespoons rendered duck fat
   (see recipe page 176)
2 leeks, minced
1 carrot, minced
1 ½ pounds fresh pumpkin flesh,
   cubed

8 cups whole milk
Salt and freshly ground black
   pepper to taste
1 tablespoon chopped parsley

Heat the duck fat in a large soup pot over medium heat. Add the leeks, stir well, cover, and cook over low heat for 15 minutes. Do not brown them. Add the carrot and cook, covered, for another 10 minutes.

Add the cubed pumpkin to the pot, then the milk. Season with salt and pepper. Bring to a boil, lower the heat, and cook, partially covered, for 45 minutes, or until the pumpkin is very tender.

Purée the soup in the bowl of a food processor or blender until smooth. Pour the soup back into a saucepan and heat it over a medium flame. If the soup is too thick, thin with a little milk. Serve the soup in a soup terrine or in a pumpkin shell that has been used to cook foie gras (see recipe page 35). Sprinkle with chopped parsley and serve.   [*Yield: 8 servings*]

SALADS AND
VEGETABLES

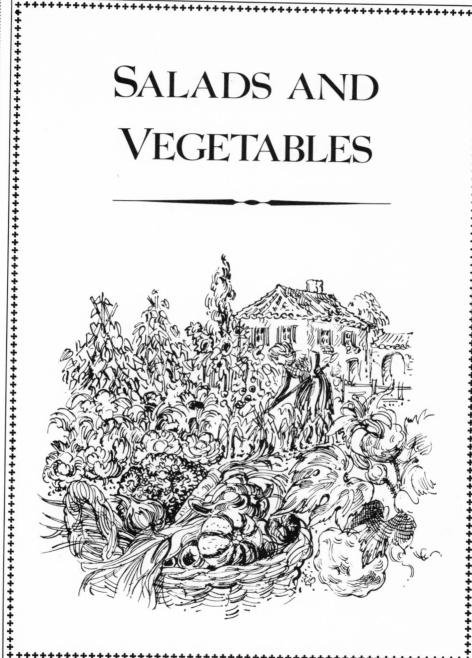

Salade à l'Aile de Perdreau Rosée et à la Cuisse Confite

PARTRIDGE SALAD

3 partridges, about 18 ounces each

2 tablespoons vegetable oil

1 tablespoon coarse salt

2 cups rendered duck fat (see recipe page 176)

4 garlic cloves, peeled

¾ teaspoon quatre épices (see recipe page 175)

6 cups loosely packed, mixed lettuces such as chicory, Boston lettuce, romaine, or radicchio

Salt and freshly ground white pepper to taste

2 shallots, minced

1 tablespoon red wine vinegar

2 tablespoons unsalted butter, cut into small cubes

The day before serving this salad, cut the partridges into serving pieces—the legs first, then the breasts with the wings attached. Remove the meat from the breast bones. Place the breast meat in a bowl and coat with the vegetable oil. Place the legs in another bowl and coat with the coarse salt. Cover both bowls and refrigerate overnight.

The next day, melt the duck fat over medium heat in a heavy pot large enough to hold the legs. Add the garlic and *quatre épices* to the pot. Wipe off the coarse salt from the legs and dry thoroughly. When the fat is warm but not hot, add the legs to the pot and cook, uncovered, for 1¼ to 1½ hours over low heat. The fat should be simmering but not boiling or the legs will fry. When the legs are cooked and can be easily pierced with the tip of a knife, remove from the fat and keep them warm. Strain the fat and reserve.

When ready to serve, clean and rinse the lettuces, and arrange on six serving plates. Remove the breasts from the refrigerator, wipe off the oil, and season them with salt and pepper. Heat ¼ cup of the reserved duck fat in a large frying pan and sauté the breasts over medium-high heat for 3 to 4 minutes on each side, or until the skin is golden. Do not overcook the meat or it will be dry. Arrange the breasts on the lettuces along with the legs. Stir the shallots into the pan and cook briefly for 1 minute. Add the vinegar and bring to a boil. Whisk in the butter a small piece at a time until it is all incorporated. Spoon the sauce over the salad and serve immediately. [*Yield: 6 servings*]

Salade d'Endives au Foie Gras

ENDIVE AND FOIE GRAS SALAD

5 large endives
Salt and freshly ground white
  pepper to taste

1 small foie gras, about 1 pound
3 tablespoons red wine vinegar
3 tablespoons white wine

Clean and rinse the endives and divide the leaves among ten serving plates. Sprinkle the leaves with salt and pepper. Cut the foie gras into twelve slices (eight in the big lobe and four in the small one) and sprinkle them with salt and pepper.

Over a high flame, heat a pan large enough to hold the foie gras slices in one layer. Add the slices and cook them briefly, about 30 seconds on each side. Remove the slices from the pan and place them on the prepared salad plates. Quickly deglaze the pan with the vinegar and white wine, bring to a boil, and cook for 30 seconds. Spoon the sauce over the foie gras and serve immediately.   [*Yield: 10 servings*]

Salade de Foie de Veau aux Épinards

CALF'S LIVER AND SPINACH SALAD

$\frac{3}{4}$ *pound calf's liver*
Salt and freshly ground black
  pepper to taste
60 small, tender spinach leaves
6 tablespoons rendered duck fat
  (see recipe page 176)

$\frac{1}{2}$ *cup white wine*
$\frac{1}{4}$ *cup sherry wine vinegar*
2 tablespoons unsalted butter, cut
  into small cubes

Cut the liver diagonally into slices about $\frac{1}{2}$ inch thick. Sprinkle with salt and pepper, and set aside. Rinse and thoroughly drain the spinach leaves and arrange them on six warmed serving plates.

Heat the duck fat in a large frying pan over medium-high heat, add the liver and sauté quickly, 30 seconds on each side. The liver should be pink inside. Arrange the liver slices on the spinach leaves and keep warm. Deglaze the pan with the wine and the vinegar, then bring to a boil. While the sauce is boiling, quickly whisk in the butter a small piece at a time. When the butter is completely incorporated, spoon the sauce over the liver and spinach, and serve immediately.   [*Yield: 6 servings*]

The Gascon Farm

The size of a family holdings varies greatly throughout the region. In the lowlands of Armagnac and Landes, farms can spread over several hundred acres or several thousand, in the case of the larger vineyards. In the high Pyrenees, farming is confined to valleys and the mountain pastures are used for grazing. The traditional Gascon farmhouse was a very modest affair—a tiny, low, and often single room, housing two or three generations of the family. Furnishings were equally Spartan, usually consisting of several benches, a few rickety tables, and earthenware utensils. Today the farmhouse is often a large, two-story building constructed of the local yellow fieldstone and topped with a mansard roof of terra-cotta tiles.

As in all agricultural enterprises, chores, divided between husband and wife, run a cycle of seasons. Spring is the time for raking, manuring, and ploughing—generally, preparing the fields; when this is done, the farmer commences planting. This is supplemented by lamb slaughtering, milking chores, and subsequent cheese production. Spring is also the time Gascon women begin raising the ducks and geese destined to become foie gras and *magret*. Summer brings haymaking, gardening, and mushroom gathering. Autumn brings the harvest of maize, apples, and nuts—primarily walnuts, hazelnuts, and chestnuts. This is also harvest time for wine and Armagnac grapes. The men, if so inclined, will take their dogs to hunt for venison, wild boar, and game birds to be sold to local restaurants or shipped to cities. The women start

selling their foie gras and fatted ducks and geese at the local market.

The Gascon garden is kept well stocked with vegetables for the household and to be sold at various markets. Typically, you might find leeks, peppers, garlic, cabbage, onions, haricot beans, and potatoes. Although modernization has come to Southwest France, for some farmers in the more remote villages of the Bearn and the Basque country, plowing and other heavy chores are still accomplished using animal and man power—oftentimes because the terrain is too rugged to permit machinery. The Gascon farmer— weather-brown skin, topped by his beret, driving his team of long-horned oxen along the rows of a hillside field—is still a common, somehow comforting, sight throughout the Gascon countryside.

Salade Frisée au Confit de Canard

DUCK CONFIT AND CHICORY SALAD

3 duck legs confit (see page 46)
1 head chicory
Salt and freshly ground black
*   pepper to taste*

6 tablespoons rendered duck fat
*   (see recipe page 176)*
4 garlic cloves, minced
2 tablespoons red wine vinegar

Preheat the oven to 350 degrees.

Place the duck legs on a baking sheet and bake in the oven for 30 minutes, or until they are golden and crispy. Meanwhile, rinse and drain the chicory thoroughly. Divide the chicory among six serving plates. Season lightly with salt and pepper.

Remove the legs from the oven and cut them in half to make six pieces. Remove the bones and shred the meat into long, wide strips. Arrange the meat and the crisp skin on the lettuce.

Heat the duck fat in a small frying pan over medium-high heat. Add the garlic and cook for 2 minutes, making sure it does not burn. Stir in the vinegar and bring to a boil quickly. Remove from the heat and spoon the warm dressing over the duck and lettuce. Serve immediately.   [*Yield: 6 servings*]

La Daube de Cèpes au Vin Blanc

CÈPES STEWED IN WHITE WINE

This dish makes a hearty, flavorful appetizer, or it can be served as a side dish to a roasted meat. Choose medium-size cèpes that are firm to the touch.

Cèpes don't like pepper in high doses, so do not use too much; it will ruin the dish.

3 pounds fresh cèpes
3 tablespoons rendered duck fat
    (see recipe page 176)
Salt to taste
$\frac{1}{4}$ pound prosciutto, finely
    chopped

6 garlic cloves, finely chopped
$\frac{1}{2}$ cup finely chopped parsley
$1\frac{1}{2}$ cups dry white wine
1 cup hot water
Freshly ground black pepper to
    taste

Wash and thoroughly dry the cèpes. Cut off the stems from the caps and reserve. Heat the duck fat in a heavy pot over medium heat. Place the cèpe caps upside down in the pot and cook over medium heat for 30 minutes. Remove the mushrooms from the pot and season with salt.

Finely chop the mushroom stems and add to the pot with the prosciutto, garlic, and parsley. Stir well and sauté over medium-high heat until the mixture starts to turn golden. Add the wine to the pot and season with salt and sparingly with pepper. As soon as the wine starts to boil, add the hot water. Carefully return the mushroom caps to the pot and cook, covered, over low heat for $1\frac{1}{2}$ hours. The mixture should not be too dry; add some hot water to the pan, if necessary, to moisten it and prevent it from burning. Serve hot. [Yield: 6 servings]

SEAFOOD

Milieu de Saumon à la Vapeur et à la Moutarde

STEAMED SALMON WITH MUSTARD

3 cups white wine

1 cup red wine vinegar

4 cups water

2 medium carrots, chopped

2 onions, chopped

8 garlic cloves, peeled

1 tablespoon herbes de Provence (see note)

½ pound unsalted butter (2 sticks), softened

⅔ cup Dijon-style mustard

1 center-cut salmon fillet, about 4 pounds

Salt and freshly ground black pepper to taste

1 pound tender green beans, trimmed

In the bottom part of a *couscoussier* or a steamer, combine the wine, vinegar, water, carrots, onions, garlic, and herbs. Bring to a boil over high heat and simmer for 5 minutes.

Combine the butter with the mustard in a small mixing bowl. Sprinkle the salmon with salt and pepper, and use half of the mustard-butter mixture to coat the salmon on both sides. Reserve the other half of the mixture.

Place the salmon on top of a *couscoussier* or a steamer, cover, and cook for 20 minutes. Arrange the green beans around the salmon and steam for 10 minutes more. Turn off the heat and let stand, covered, for 10 minutes.

Arrange the salmon on a serving platter with the green beans around it, and serve the remaining mustard-butter on the side. [*Yield: 8 servings*]

NOTE: *Herbes de Provence* is a commercial blend of dried herbs, available in many specialty food shops. It includes thyme, fennel, bay leaf, basil, and rosemary.

Salmon

Spilling off the Pyrenees is a network of torrents, fast-running, glacier-formed streams known as *gaves*. Their proximity to the sea makes the *gaves* a favorite spawning ground for the Atlantic salmon, which at times have choked these waters in their upstream return to the fresh-water pools where they were hatched. Adour, a small river in the southwestern corner of Gascony, was one such well-stocked salmon route during the Middle Ages. The fish was in fact so plentiful that laborers, on farms bordering the Adour, had it written into their contract that they should not be fed salmon for supper more than twice per week.

Escalope de Saumon Grillée
dans Sa Peau au Gros Sel

SALMON FILLET GRILLED IN ITS SKIN

The key to this simple recipe is to leave the scales of the fish on the skin. As the fish cooks, the scales will burn and give a smoky flavor to the flesh. Ask the fishmonger to leave the scales on.

2 salmon fillets, about 2 pounds each with scales on the skin   *4 teaspoons coarse salt*

Cut each fillet into four pieces, about $\frac{1}{2}$ pound each. Heat a large nonstick frying pan over medium-high flame. When the pan is very hot, add fish fillets skin side down. Sprinkle the flesh generously with the salt and cook for 10 to 11 minutes, until firm to the touch. Do not worry if skin appears to burn. The flesh on top of the fish may not look sufficiently cooked, but it will be.

Remove the fillets from the pan and arrange on individual serving plates, skin side down. The fish is best eaten with a spoon, which you can use to scoop up only the flesh. Serve with sweet butter on the side, if desired. [*Yield: 8 servings*]

Papillote de Saumon
Frais aux Herbes Vertes

PAPILLOTES OF SALMON AND FRESH HERBS

6 tablespoons unsalted butter ($\frac{1}{2}$ stick)

6 salmon steaks, about $\frac{1}{3}$ pound each

6 parsley sprigs, chopped

6 chervil sprigs, chopped

6 fresh tarragon leaves, chopped

3 fresh mint leaves, chopped

6 fresh marjoram leaves, chopped

3 teaspoons minced fresh chives

Salt and crushed white pepper to taste

Preheat the oven to 400 degrees.

Spread a large sheet of heavy-duty aluminum foil or parchment paper on a flat surface. Invert a 12-inch round cake pan on the foil and trace around the pan with a sharp knife to make a 12-inch circle. Repeat until you have six circles.

Place one of the circles on the work surface, rub 1 tablespoon of butter all over it, and leave any extra butter on the lower half of the circle. Place one salmon steak on top of the lower half of the circle and sprinkle one sixth of each herb all over it. Season with salt and pepper. Fold the foil over to enclose the contents, leaving a little room for expansion. Crimp to seal the foil as tightly as possible. Repeat with the remaining salmon. Place the six papillotes on a baking sheet and bake for 10 minutes. Serve immediately.   [*Yield: 6 servings*]

Chateaubriand de Thon Rouge au Beurre de Persil

TUNA STEAKS WITH PARSLEY BUTTER

6 tablespoons vegetable oil
1 tablespoon thyme
1 teaspoon tarragon
1 teaspoon rosemary
2 large tuna steaks, each about
   $1\frac{1}{2}$ pounds, and 3 inches thick

6 tablespoons unsalted butter ($\frac{3}{4}$
   stick), at room temperature
2 tablespoons minced parsley
Salt and freshly ground black
   pepper to taste

Combine 4 tablespoons of the oil with the thyme, tarragon, and rosemary. Coat the tuna steaks with the mixture and marinate in the refrigerator for 3 to 4 hours.

Meanwhile, combine the butter with the parsley in a small mixing bowl until well blended. Shape the mixture into a log, enclose it in aluminum foil, and refrigerate until ready to use. Remove the fish from the refrigerator 30 minutes before cooking to bring it to room temperature.

Preheat the oven to 400 degrees.

Heat the remaining 2 tablespoons oil in a large frying pan over high heat. Add the tuna steaks and lower the heat to medium high. Cook for 4 minutes on each side to sear the steaks. Place the pan in the oven and cook for another 4 to 5 minutes or to taste. The tuna will be medium rare. Season with salt and pepper. Cut the parsley butter into six thick slices. Cut the tuna steaks into six serving pieces, place a pat of butter on top of each, and serve immediately. French fries make the perfect accompaniment. [*Yield: 6 servings*]

Saumon à l'Ail Confit
et à la Purée d'Ail

SALMON WITH GARLIC CONFIT AND GARLIC PUREE

2 cups rendered duck fat (see
    recipe page 176)
40 garlic cloves, peeled
$\frac{3}{4}$ teaspoon quatre épices (see
    recipe page 175)
Salt and freshly ground black
    pepper to taste

6 salmon steaks, about $\frac{1}{3}$ pound
    each
Coarse salt
6 parsley sprigs

Heat the duck fat in a small saucepan over low heat. Add the garlic cloves, the *quatre épices*, salt, and pepper. Cook the garlic slowly for 25 minutes. The fat should barely simmer, not boil. When the garlic is soft, drain and set aside the six best looking garlic cloves for garnish and puree the remaining ones.

Season the salmon steaks with salt and pepper, and steam for 8 minutes, or until the flesh is firm to the touch.

To serve, spoon some garlic puree over each of six warmed dinner plates, place the salmon on top, sprinkle with a little coarse salt, and garnish with a garlic clove and a parsley sprig. [*Yield: 6 servings*]

Bar à l'Armagnac et au Vin Rouge

SEA BASS IN ARMAGNAC AND RED WINE SAUCE

3 whole sea bass, about 2 pounds
    each
24 pearl onions, peeled
½ cup flour
Salt and freshly ground black
    pepper to taste
½ cup rendered duck fat (see
    recipe page 176)

¼ pound slab prosciutto, cut into
    ½-inch cubes
12 mushrooms, quartered
2 cups Zinfandel or other strong
    red wine
½ cup Armagnac
4 tablespoons unsalted butter (½
    stick), cut into small cubes

Have your fishmonger scale and clean each fish, leaving the head and tail on.

Bring some lightly salted water to a boil and blanch the pearl onions for 5 minutes. Drain and set aside until ready to use.

Rinse the fish and pat dry with paper towels. Combine the flour with some salt and pepper on a flat plate and dredge the fish lightly in it. Heat the duck fat over high heat in a frying pan large enough to hold the fish comfortably or in two smaller pans. When the fat starts to smoke, add the fish to the pan, lower the heat to medium, and cook for 5 minutes on each side. Remove the fish from the pan and keep warm until ready to serve.

Pour off the fat from the pan, leaving about 1 tablespoon. Add the onions, prosciutto, and mushrooms and sauté for 5 minutes, stirring occasionally, or until golden. Pour in the Zinfandel and the Armagnac, and reduce over high heat to 1 cup. Season with salt and pepper if necessary. Whisk in the butter, a few pieces at a time, until it is all incorporated. Spoon the sauce over the fish and scatter the onions, prosciutto, and mushrooms around it. Serve immediately. [*Yield: 6 servings*]

Red Snapper au Cabernet Sauvignon

POACHED RED SNAPPER IN CABERNET SAUVIGNON

6 medium leeks

2 cups cabernet sauvignon, or other good red wine

4 shallots, finely chopped

6 red snapper fillets, about 6 ounces each

Salt and freshly ground black pepper to taste

6 tablespoons unsalted butter ($\frac{3}{4}$ stick), cut into small cubes

Trim the leeks, leaving the white parts only, and rinse them well. Cut them crosswise into 1-inch pieces. Bring some lightly salted water to a boil and blanch the leeks for 10 minutes. Drain and set aside until ready to use.

Heat the wine in a small saucepan. Meanwhile, spread 1 tablespoon of butter in a frying pan large enough to hold all the fillets (or two smaller pans if necessary), spread the shallots over the bottom and place the fish over them. Sprinkle the leeks over the fish and season with salt and pepper. Pour over the boiling wine and cook for 6 minutes over medium-high heat. Remove the fillets and the leeks from the pan and arrange on warmed serving plates. Keep warm until ready to serve.

Reduce the sauce over high heat by about one half. Whisk in the remaining cubes of butter, a few pieces at a time, until it is all incorporated and the sauce is smooth. Taste and adjust the seasoning with salt and pepper, and spoon the sauce over the fish. Serve immediately.   [*Yield: 6 servings*]

Brochettes de Saumon Grillé au Magret Fumé et aux Champignons

BROCHETTES OF SALMON, SMOKED MAGRET, AND MUSHROOMS

1 salmon fillet, about 2 pounds
1 smoked magret, about ¾ pound,
 or a quality bacon
18 mushroom caps
Salt and freshly ground black
 pepper to taste

4 shallots, finely chopped
¾ cup white wine
4 tablespoons unsalted butter (½
 stick), cut into small pieces

Preheat the broiler.

Cut the salmon into 1½-inch cubes, leaving the skin on. Cut the *magret* into ⅛-inch-thick slices about ½ inch long, leaving the skin on. Oil six long skewers and arrange the *magret*, fish, and mushroom caps on them, starting with the *magret*. Use four pieces of each. Repeat until all the ingredients are used. Season the brochettes with salt and pepper, and arrange on a lightly buttered baking sheet. Broil for 3 minutes on each side or to taste.

Remove the skewers from the broiler and keep warm. Add the shallots to the pan and deglaze with the wine. Transfer the mixture to a saucepan and reduce over high heat by two thirds. Whisk in the butter, a few pieces at a time, until it is all incorporated, and then spoon the sauce over the brochettes. Serve immediately.   [*Yield: 6 servings*]

Rôti d'Huitre au Magret Fumé

TOASTS OF OYSTERS AND SMOKED MAGRET

This recipe should be served as an hors d'oeuvre.

18 oysters
1 smoked magret, about ¾ pound
⅓ to ½ cup heavy cream

1 French baguette, cut into 18 slices
3 tablespoons unsalted butter

Shuck the oysters and reserve their liquor. Remove and discard the skin from the *magret* and halve the remaining meat. Cut one half of the *magret* into small cubes; slice the other half into eighteen pieces.

Place the *magret* cubes in the bowl of a food processor along with ⅓ cup of cream and the reserved oyster liquor. Puree to a smooth thick paste. (The amount of cream you use will depend on how much oyster liquor you have; start with ⅓ cup and increase the amount as needed.)

Preheat the broiler.

Lightly toast the bread slices. Spread with butter on one side. Spread a generous layer of *magret* puree and top with one slice of *magret* and one oyster.

Arrange the toasts on a baking sheet and broil for 1½ to 2 minutes. Spread more of the puree on top and return to the broiler for a few seconds, just to warm. Serve immediately.   [*Yield: 6 servings*]

Écrevisses Sautées au Jambon et au Chenin Blanc

SAUTÉED CRAYFISH AND HAM IN CHENIN BLANC

36 to 42 crayfish
3 tablespoons vegetable oil
¾ cup Armagnac
3 carrots, finely chopped
3 medium onions, finely chopped
6 ounces cured ham, such as
　prosciutto, finely chopped

1 sprig tarragon
Salt and freshly ground white
　pepper to taste
Approximately 2 cups Chenin
　Blanc wine

Rinse the crayfish under cold running water. Remove the intestinal veins by firmly twisting the middle tail fin and pulling.

Heat the oil in a large, thick-bottomed pot over a high flame. Add the crayfish and cook for 2 to 3 minutes, until their shells turn red. Add the Armagnac to the pot and flambé until the flames disappear. Be careful because Armagnac can create high flames. Stir in the carrots, onions, ham, tarragon, salt and pepper. Cook for 3 minutes, shaking the pot often. Add enough Chenin Blanc to cover the crayfish. Bring to a boil and cook for 5 minutes.

Remove the crayfish to a serving platter and keep warm. Simmer the sauce for about 8 to 10 minutes, or until it becomes thick and is reduced by half. Pour over the crayfish and serve hot. *[Yield: 6 servings]*

Morue à la Gasconne

SALTED CODFISH GASCON-STYLE

2 pounds salted codfish
1 quart milk
⅓ cup rendered duck fat (see
    recipe page 176)
4 garlic cloves, thinly sliced
2 shallots, thinly sliced

1 tablespoon chervil
1 teaspoon thyme
Salt and freshly ground black
    pepper to taste
3 large potatoes, peeled

Soak the codfish in water for 48 hours, changing the water three or four times. The fish should lose all its salt. Remove and discard the bones and skin. Cut the fish into large pieces and place in a noncorrosive pot. Pour the milk over the fish and bring to a low simmer. Cook for 15 minutes, making sure the milk does not boil. Drain the codfish and flake it lightly with a fork. Reserve the milk.

Heat 2 tablespoons of the duck fat in a large frying pan, add the garlic and shallots. Sauté briefly over medium-high heat, about 3 minutes. Add the codfish, chervil, and thyme. Cook for 5 minutes over high heat, stirring often. Place into a bowl and season with salt and pepper. Let cool. Cut the potatoes into ⅛-inch-thick slices. Heat the remaining duck fat in a large frying pan and sauté the potatoes briefly. When they start to brown, sprinkle with salt and pepper, cover, and cook over medium heat for 20 minutes, or until they are soft.

Preheat the oven to 350 degrees.

Butter a large baking dish, spread one third of the codfish puree at the bottom, layer half of the potatoes, spread another third of the cod purée, arrange the remaining potatoes, and spread the remaining cod. Pour 1 cup of the reserved milk over it. Bake for 30 minutes, or until hot and bubbly. Add some of the reserved milk during the baking time if the mixture looks too dry. [*Yield: 8 servings*]

POULTRY

Poulet à l'Ail et à l'Ail

CHICKEN WITH TWO GARLICS

2 chickens, about 3 pounds each
⅓ cup rendered duck fat (see
   recipe page 176)
10 garlic cloves, peeled
Salt and freshly ground black
   pepper to taste

1½ cups chardonnay wine
20 garlic cloves confit (see recipe
   page 177)

Cut the chickens into six pieces each (two legs, two breasts, and two wings). Cut the legs in half at the thigh joint. Reserve the carcasses for stock or soup.

In a heavy pot, heat the duck fat. Sauté the chicken pieces, a few at a time, over high heat for 5 minutes, or until golden brown on both sides. Remove the pieces from the pot and repeat with the remaining chicken.

When all the pieces are brown, return to the pot along with the fresh garlic cloves. Lower the heat and season well with salt and pepper. Cook, covered, 12 minutes for the breast, 15 minutes for the wings, and 20 minutes for the legs. Remove the pieces when cooked and keep them warm while the rest finish cooking.

Discard the fat from the pot, add the garlic *confit*, and deglaze with the chardonnay. Cook over medium-high heat, smashing the cloves, until the garlic forms a smooth purée, about 8 minutes. Pour the garlic purée over the chicken and serve with thinly sliced potatoes, sautéed in duck fat.   [*Yield: 6 servings*]

Petit Poulet Grillé à la Moutarde

GRILLED CHICKEN WITH MUSTARD

4 tablespoons unsalted butter ($\frac{1}{2}$ stick), at room temperature
2 tablespoons strong Dijon-style mustard
2 teaspoons dried thyme
3 teaspoons fresh mint

Salt and freshly ground black pepper to taste
1 small chicken, about $2\frac{3}{4}$ pounds
1 pound broccoli, broken into stalks

In a small mixing bowl combine the butter with the mustard, herbs, salt, and pepper. Set aside but do not refrigerate.

Place the chicken, breast side up, on a board. Using a sharp knife, cut through the skin and the flesh along the ridge of the breast bone. Starting on one side, run the knife between the bone and the flesh, scrapping and pulling the meat. Cut through the joint of the shoulder to release the wing from the carcass. Repeat on the other side. Remove and discard the carcass being careful not to separate the two breasts. Flatten the meat slightly by pounding it with a mallet or the bottom of a heavy saucepan. Rub the mustard mixture all over the chicken, then place on a baking sheet. Let it stand for 1 hour.

Preheat the broiler.

Place the chicken on the top shelf of the oven under the broiler and cook for 10 minutes. Lower the shelf and cook for another 10 minutes, or until the chicken is golden brown and the juices run clear when the meat is pierced. Keep the chicken in a warm place and pour the cooking juices into a frying pan.

Meanwhile, bring a large pot of salted water to a boil. Add the broccoli, bring back to a boil, and cook for 5 minutes. Drain. Heat the cooking juices and add the broccoli. Sauté briefly just to warm through. Serve immediately with the chicken.   [*Yield: 2 servings*]

Chicken

In 817 at the council of Aix-la-Chapelle, Charlemagne decreed that monks could eat poultry only at Easter and Christmas; and through the ages, chicken remained something of a delicacy. André Daguin attests: "In 1884–85 the most expensive item on my grandfather's menu was chicken."

The meat of Gascon chickens has a warm golden color not found in their northern brethren. Some of Columbus' Basque crew returned to their native Pyrenees and the maize they brought from the new world crept down the northern slopes to feed the poultry of the Southwest, producing this deeper color.

Despite their rarified diet, Daguin observes that his chickens "ask for a little attention. I've found that when roasting a chicken, the breast is always cooked when the legs are not yet perfectly done, then the breast gets dry by the time the legs are ready."

Daguin's solution? "Cook the breast and legs separately. Each part can be sautéed, roasted, or grilled. Another idea is to cook each part in its own style and serve it in its own sauce." If you are a purist and only roasted chicken will do, cook the chicken until the legs are just done; then, let it rest in the warm oven with the tail up for a few minutes. The juices will flow down to moisten the breast. This technique can also apply to roast a turkey: Finish the cooking time breast side down.

Pigeon à l'Ail et au Merlot

SQUABS WITH GARLIC AND MERLOT WINE SAUCE

18 garlic cloves, peeled
6 squabs, about 1 pound each
Salt and freshly ground black
    pepper to taste

$\frac{1}{3}$ cup rendered duck fat, heated
    (see recipe page 176)
2 cups Merlot wine
$\frac{1}{4}$ cup heavy cream

Blanch the garlic cloves in boiling water for 10 minutes. Drain. Preheat the oven to 450 degrees.

Rinse the squabs and dry them inside and out with paper towels. Stuff two garlic cloves inside each squab and season with salt and pepper, inside and outside. Place the birds in a roasting pan just large enough to hold them in one layer. Rub the duck fat all over them. Roast the squabs in the oven for 20 minutes, basting three or four times during the cooking time. Remove from the oven and keep the squabs warm.

Skim off the fat from the roasting pan with a spoon. Deglaze the pan with the wine, scraping the bottom to get up every browned bit of meat. Pour the liquid into a small saucepan, add the remaining garlic, and reduce by half. Add the cream, reduce over high heat, without stirring, for 2 to 3 minutes, or until the sauce starts to thicken and is well blended. Spoon the sauce over the squabs and serve immediately. A rice pilaf makes a very good side dish. Do not forget to provide finger bowls, as the squabs have small bones and you will have to eat them with your fingers.   [*Yield: 6 servings*]

Deux Cailles, Deux Sauces

TWO QUAILS, TWO SAUCES

6 tablespoons vegetable oil
12 quails, about 4 ounces each
1 tablespoon strong Dijon-style
   mustard
1 tablespoon old-fashioned grainy
   mustard
1 tablespoon unsalted butter, at
   room temperature
½ teaspoon thyme

½ teaspoon rosemary
Salt and freshly ground black
   pepper to taste
3 tablespoons rendered duck fat
   (see recipe page 176)
18 seedless green grapes, peeled
1 cup white wine
½ cup chicken stock
⅓ cup heavy cream

Two or three hours before cooking, rub the oil over six of the quails and marinate them at room temperature. Meanwhile, in a small mixing bowl, combine the two mustards, butter, dried herbs, salt, and pepper. When ready to cook, spread the mixture all over the marinated quails to coat well.

Sprinkle the remaining quails with salt and pepper. Heat the duck fat in a heavy saucepan and sauté the remaining quails over high heat until they are golden brown on both sides. Lower the heat to medium, cover, and cook for 10 minutes. Remove the quails from the pan and keep them warm. Discard the fat, stir in the grapes, deglaze with the wine, and reduce by half. Add the chicken stock and reduce again by half. Add the cream and reduce by one fourth. Season to taste with salt and pepper. Keep the sauce warm until ready to serve.

Preheat the broiler.

Place the six mustard-coated quails on a baking sheet and grill for 3 to 4 minutes on each side.

To serve, arrange some sauce on each of six warmed dinner plates and place a sautéed and a grilled quail on each plate. Garnish with the grapes and serve immediately. Steamed spinach makes a good side dish. [*Yield: 6 servings*]

Canettes Sautées au Fumet de Champignons

SAUTÉED DUCK WITH MUSHROOM SAUCE

2 ducks, about 4 pounds each
1 carrot, coarsely chopped
2 onions, coarsely chopped
2 celery stalks, coarsely chopped
1 bouquet garni consisting of 1
    bay leaf, 6 parsley sprigs, 1
    teaspoon thyme, 10
    peppercorns
Salt and freshly ground black
    pepper to taste

2 tablespoons rendered duck fat
    (see recipe page 176)
1 shallot, minced
1 cup white wine
$\frac{1}{3}$ cup heavy cream
$\frac{1}{4}$ pound mushrooms, cut into
    thin slices
2 tablespoons unsalted butter

Cut the ducks into serving pieces, two breasts and two thighs with the legs attached, using a sharp boning knife, cutting away from the breastbone. Refrigerate the breasts and the thighs until ready to use. Remove and discard any fat from the carcasses.

Place the duck carcasses, the wings, and the necks in a stockpot. Add the carrot, onions, celery, and bouquet garni. Cover with 8 cups of water, bring to a boil, and cook for 2 hours over medium-low heat, frequently skimming off the fat. Pass the stock through a fine sieve, return to a saucepan, and reduce to 2 cups. Remove from the heat and reserve until ready to use.

Sprinkle the duck pieces with salt and pepper. Heat the duck fat in a large sauté pan over high heat. Add the duck pieces, skin side down, and cook, covered, over medium-high heat, 4 to 5 minutes. Turn over and cook, covered, for another 4 minutes for the breasts and 12 to 15 minutes for the thighs. They should be golden brown on both sides. Remove from the pan and keep warm until ready to serve. Discard the fat, stir in the shallots, and deglaze with the wine. Reduce by half over high heat. Add the reserved duck stock and reduce by half over medium heat. Stir in the cream and reduce to one cup.

Meanwhile, sauté the mushrooms in the butter over high heat for 3 minutes. Remove with a slotted spoon and add to the sauce. Season to taste with salt and pepper, spoon over the duck pieces, and serve immediately. [*Yield: 6 servings*]

Pigeons Poêlés au Vinaigre de Romarin

SAUTÉED SQUABS WITH ROSEMARY VINEGAR

Fifteen days before you plan to serve this recipe, add four sprigs of fresh rosemary to a bottle of red wine vinegar. Set the bottle aside in a cool place until ready to use.

6 squabs, about 1 pound each	1 shallot, finely chopped
Salt and freshly ground black pepper to taste	1/4 cup rosemary vinegar
14 tablespoons unsalted butter (1¾ sticks)	12 young leeks, steamed

Cut each squab into six serving pieces: the legs, the breasts, and the wings. Reserve the carcasses to use later in stocks or soups. Set the livers and hearts aside until ready to cook.

Season each piece of squab with salt and pepper on both sides. In a large frying pan, heat 4 tablespoons of the butter over medium-high heat. Cook the legs 5 minutes on each side. Add the breasts and wings to the pan and cook them 7 to 10 minutes, to taste. (Squab breast is usually served rare or medium rare.) Remove the pieces from the pan and keep warm until ready to serve. Meanwhile, in a small frying pan, heat 2 tablespoons of butter and sauté the hearts and livers for 2 minutes. Set aside with the squabs.

Pour off the fat from the skillet in which the squabs were cooked. Sauté the shallot for two minutes and deglaze with the vinegar. Reduce by half and whisk in the remaining butter, a few small pieces at a time until all incorporated. To serve, arrange two legs, two breasts, two wings, and one heart and liver on each serving plate. Spoon the sauce over the pieces and garnish with two leeks.   [*Yield: 6 servings*]

Poule au Pot à la Gasconne

POULE AU POT GASCON-STYLE

1 pound chicken carcasses and
  necks
1 gallon water
½ pound prosciutto, finely
  chopped
4 garlic cloves, finely chopped
2 shallots, finely chopped
¼ pound chicken livers, finely
  chopped
1 cup finely chopped bread
2 eggs
Salt and freshly ground black
  pepper to taste

1 large roaster chicken, about 6
  pounds
2 onions, peeled
3 cloves
6 leeks
3 large carrots
1 small cabbage, quartered
3 turnips
Caper and cornichon sauce (see
  recipe page 160)

In a large pot, combine the carcasses with the water. Bring to a boil, lower
the heat to medium, and simmer for 1 hour. Strain the liquid through a fine
sieve and return it to the pot. Bring the broth to a low simmer.

In a small mixing bowl combine the prosciutto, garlic, shallots, chicken
livers, bread, and eggs. Season with a little salt (depending on the saltiness
of the ham) and pepper. Stuff the chicken with the mixture and truss it.

Preheat the broiler.

Halve one onion. Place it under the broiler and grill until the surface
becomes very dark, almost burned. Stick the cloves in the remaining onion.

Place the chicken and the onions into the simmering broth, adding more
water if necessary to cover the fowl. Bring to a boil and cook for 15 minutes,
skimming off the fat. Reduce the heat to a simmer and cook for 1¼ to 1½
hours.

Trim, clean, and tie the leeks together. Peel and rinse the other vegetables.
Half an hour before the end of the cooking time, add the vegetables to the
pot and season with salt and pepper. Bring to a boil, lower the heat to a
simmer, and cook until the vegetables are tender and the chicken is done.
Add more water if necessary during the cooking time.

Serve the degreased broth as a first course. Cut the chicken into serving
pieces and arrange them on a platter with the vegetables and the stuffing.
Serve with the caper and cornichons sauce on the side.   [Yield: 6 servings]

Henri IV and a Chicken in Every Pot

Whether conquering seasoned armies, self-righteous bigots, or reluctant mistresses, Gascony's own Henri d'Albret (1553–1610) attacked every problem with enormous will and enthusiasm. The Bearnais proudly claim this as a result of his upbringing in the Pyrenean foothills.

Henri's most famous quotation is gastronomic as well as political in nature. He said "I want no peasant in my kingdom to be so poor that he cannot eat meat on weekdays and put a chicken in his pot every Sunday."

The pot to which he was referring was a huge iron affair hung over the hearth on its *crémaillère,* a hook which could be swung in and out of the fireplace. It was during Henri's time that a great revolution was brewing over what exactly should be dropped into the pot along with the chicken.

Chief fomenter of this revolution was Olivier de Serres (1539–1619) whose brace of books on farming, *Théâtre de l'Agriculture* and *Ménage de Champs* (both published in 1600 at the suggestion of Henri), were the result of experiments on his estate at Pradel. Henri was a great admirer of de Serres, who was almost solely responsible for the use of expertly cultivated vegetables in stews, and casseroles on the French table.

Pintades à l'Ail-Citron

GUINEA HENS WITH A GARLIC-LEMON SAUCE

The garlic and the lemon play off one another in an intriguing fashion in this unconventional dish. Subtle it is not, so only garlic lovers and lemon fanciers need try. If this sauce suits your tastes, try it with all kinds of poultry. In this recipe we use guinea hen, a bird with a firm, meaty texture and distinctive, though not gamey, flavor.

2 large heads garlic
1 lemon
Coarse salt to taste
½ cup heavy cream
2 guinea hens, 2½ to 3 pounds each

Salt and freshly ground black pepper to taste
2 tablespoons vegetable oil
1 carrot, cut into chunks
1 onion, cut into chunks
¼ cup port wine

Peel the garlic cloves and remove any green sprouts from the center of each clove.

Using a vegetable peeler, remove the zest from the lemon. With a small sharp paring knife, scrape off all the white pith from the lemon and discard. Thinly slice the lemon. Discard the seeds.

Place the zest into a small saucepan filled with cold water.

Bring to a boil and blanch for 1 minute. Drain.

Place the lemon slices, the zest, the garlic, and a large pinch of coarse salt in a small, heavy saucepan. Cover with cold water and bring to a boil. Reduce heat and let simmer, covered, for 2½ hours, adding more water when it is almost dry. Do not let the mixture burn. From time to time break the garlic and lemon into pieces with a wooden spoon. The mixture will become light brown and thick. The garlic will turn into a puree and the lemon will break into small chunks.

Add the cream to the pan while stirring with a wooden spoon, and reduce by a quarter. (This sauce can be made a day ahead, covered with plastic wrap, and refrigerated.)

Preheat the oven to 400 degrees.

Season the guinea hens with salt and pepper, inside and outside. Truss the birds and rub the oil over them. Scatter the onion and carrot in a roasting pan large enough to hold both birds. Place the guinea hens, one breast down and roast for 15 minutes. Turn the hens on their other breast and roast for

another 15 minutes. Reduce the heat to 350 degrees, turn the birds breast side up, and roast for 30 to 35 minutes.

Meanwhile, heat the garlic-lemon sauce over low heat. Remove the birds from the oven and let rest, breast side down, in a warm place. Discard the fat from the roasting pan and deglaze with the port wine over medium high heat, scraping the bottom of the pan. Pass the sauce through a fine sieve and return it to a saucepan. Add the warmed garlic-lemon sauce and cook for 3 minutes over medium heat. Stir in the juices from the guinea hens.

Carve the guinea hens into serving pieces and serve with the sauce on the side.   [*Yield: 6 servings*]

Portefeuille de Poitrine de Dinde au Roquefort et Sauternes

TURKEY AND ROQUEFORT SCALOPPINE WITH SAUTERNES SAUCE

Turkey parts are becoming more widely available in American supermarkets. They are versatile and inexpensive, and combine well with all sorts of ingredients. This Gascon recipe is exceptionally good.

6 5-ounce scaloppines from fresh turkey breast
Salt and freshly ground black pepper to taste
6 ounces Roquefort cheese

3 tablespoons unsalted butter
1 shallot, minced
½ cup Sauternes
6 tablespoons Roquefort butter (see recipe page 178), chilled

Place the individual turkey scaloppines between sheets of plastic wrap. Flatten them as thinly as possible with a meat pounder. Put the scaloppines on a work surface. Sprinkle them with salt and pepper.

Spread about 1 ounce of Roquefort cheese on one half of each slice and fold the other half over to form a pocket. Press down to seal the pocket.

Heat the butter in a heavy skillet and cook the scaloppines over medium-high heat until golden, about 4 minutes on each side. Remove them from the skillet and keep warm.

Pour off the fat from the pan, stir in the minced shallot, and deglaze the pan with the Sauternes. Reduce the wine over medium heat for 5 minutes. Whisk little pieces of cold Roquefort butter into the pan to make a smooth homogeneous sauce. Adjust the seasonings. Arrange the turkey pockets on a serving platter and spoon the hot sauce over it. Serve immediately. [*Yield: 6 servings*]

MEAT

Pot-au-Feu de Jarret de Boeuf en Gelée

COLD POT-AU-FEU OF BEEF SHANKS IN ASPIC

This dish is time-consuming but worth the effort. Start three days before you plan to serve it.

4 pounds center-cut beef shank	2 calves' feet
2 heads garlic	1 bouquet garni consisting of 1
$\frac{1}{3}$ cup coarse salt	teaspoon dried thyme, 1 bay
6 small carrots, peeled	leaf, 8 sprigs parsley, and 10
4 small turnips, peeled	black peppercorns
8 small leeks, cleaned and	3 quarts cold water
trimmed	$\frac{1}{4}$ pound green beans
4 celery stalks	2 cups Madeira wine
$2\frac{1}{2}$ pounds brisket	5 tarragon leaves

Two days before cooking the *pot-au-feu,* place the beef shank in a pot of cold water, bring just to a boil, and drain. Cool under cold running water to wash off any fat residue and grizzle. Dry with paper towels. Place the shank on a baking sheet. Cut one of the garlic heads crosswise and rub the meat all over with it. Rub some of the coarse salt on the meat. Cover the meat and refrigerate for 24 hours, rubbing it with the salt and garlic three or four times during the day. Wipe off excess salt when ready to cook.

Place two carrots, two turnips, two leeks and the celery in a large stockpot along with the shank, calves' feet, bouquet garni, and cold water. Bring to a slow simmer, skim off the fat, and cook, covered, for 3 hours. Pass the stock through a fine sieve, reserving the stock. Do not discard the vegetables and the meat; they make an excellent cold lunch, served as a salad with a shallot vinaigrette. Degrease the stock thoroughly. Refrigerate until ready to use.

The next day trim the green beans and cut them in half. Cut the remaining carrots and turnips into 1$\frac{1}{2}$- by $\frac{1}{4}$-inch sticks and the leeks into 1$\frac{1}{2}$-inch-long pieces. Wrap each bunch of vegetables in cheesecloth to form little packages. Peel the remaining garlic head, remove any green sprouts from the center, and cut the cloves into thin slices. Drop the garlic slices into boiling water and blanch for 1 minute. Drain immediately. Set all the vegetables aside until ready to use.

Place a three-quart bowl in the refrigerator to chill.

Bring the beef stock back to a slow simmer over medium heat, then add

the brisket. This will seal the meat quickly, keeping the juices inside. Simmer for at least 4 hours, or until the meat is very tender.

Half an hour before the end of the cooking time, add the vegetable packages to the stock. Cook the carrot and green bean packages for 10 minutes, and the turnips and leeks for 6 to 8 minutes. Remove as they cook and set aside. Remove and discard the cheesecloth.

When the meat is cooked, remove it from the pot and set aside to cool. Line a fine sieve or a *chinois* with a clean linen towel and pour the stock through it.

Pour the stock back into the pot and add the Madeira. Reduce, over a high flame, to 1 quart and let cool. Taste and adjust the seasonings of the stock. It should be well seasoned with salt and pepper.

Cut the meat into 1-inch cubes. When the meat, the vegetables, and the stock are at room temperature, remove the bowl from the refrigerator and pour ½ cup of stock into it. Return the bowl to the refrigerator for a few minutes until the stock has solidified.

Place the garlic slices, tarragon leaves, carrot and turnip sticks, green beans, leeks and meat cubes on a work surface. Arrange the tarragon leaves at the bottom of the bowl with a few slices of garlic. Arrange the meat, vegetables and remaining garlic in layers, mixing them evenly. Do not push on the layers to pack the ingredients or the stock will not be able to go through the layers. Fill the bowl with the stock and place in the refrigerator overnight to set.

When ready to serve, unmold by running a knife between the aspic and the edges of the bowl. Place a serving plate on top of the bowl and invert it. Cut into wedges and serve with hot french fries and some coarse salt on the side. [*Yield: 8 servings*]

Beef

Very few traditional recipes in Gascony are made with beef. Cattle were used as farm workers—pulling plows, carts, wagons—doing all the heavy work the farmer and his familly could not do themselves. The animals were therefore an essential ingredient—alive—in the smooth working of the farm, and their owners would not have dreamed of consuming such a valuable farm "tool." If an animal was injured, and therefore unable to pull his weight (literally and figuratively), then it would be killed and consumed. But since these had been hard-working stock, bred for strength not tenderness, the few beef recipes in Gascon cuisine usually prescribe a long, slow stewing, to render the meat palatable.

Faux Filets au Beurre d'Anchois

STEAK WITH ANCHOVY BUTTER

2 2-ounce cans anchovies, packed in oil

12 tablespoons unsalted butter (1½ sticks), at room temperature

3 12- to 14-ounce tenderloin steaks, ½ inch thick, at room temperature

Freshly ground black pepper to taste

3 pounds broccoli, trimmed and cut into bite-size pieces

Remove the anchovies from the cans and drain well. Rinse them under cold running water and pat dry. Place the anchovies in the bowl of a food processor and chop finely. Add the butter to the bowl and blend well to form a smooth anchovy butter. Set aside until ready to use.

Season the steaks with pepper.

Preheat the broiler.

Bring some unsalted water to a boil in the bottom part of a steamer or a *couscoussier*. Place the broccoli in the top part and cook for 5 to 8 minutes. Remove from the steamer and keep warm until ready to serve.

Meanwhile, heat a large frying pan over a high flame. When the pan is very hot, sauté the steaks briefly, about 1 minute on each side. The outsides should be colored and the center still raw and cold. Place the steaks on a baking sheet and coat them with two-thirds of the anchovy butter. Broil for 3 minutes without turning the steaks. They will be medium rare; cook longer, to taste. Place the steaks on a heated serving platter. Melt the remaining butter on the hot baking sheet, stirring to combine with the cooking juices.

Cut the steaks into thin slices and stir the juices into the melted butter. Spoon half of the sauce over the steaks and toss the broccoli in the remaining half. Serve immediately.   [*Yield: 6 servings*]

Foie Gras,
Magret, and
Other Good Food
from Gascony

Gigot d'Agneau en Gasconnade

LEG OF LAMB GASCON-STYLE

When a meat is *en Gasconnade* (in Gascon style), it usually means some garlic and anchovies are in the dish. Garlic has always been part of Gascon cooking, and the anchovies appeared in the Middle Ages, when the government imposed a high tax on salt. The ingenious Gascons started to use salted anchovies in their cooking, creating complex and succulent dishes while avoiding the tax. The following two recipes reflect this unique Gascon style.

1 3-pound leg of lamb
8 garlic cloves, halved
12 anchovy fillets, packed in oil
Freshly ground black pepper to taste
$\frac{1}{4}$ cup rendered duck fat (see recipe page 176)

1 carrot, coarsely chopped
1 onion, coarsely chopped
1 turnip, coarsely chopped
$\frac{3}{4}$ cup dry red wine
$\frac{1}{4}$ cup anchovy butter (see recipe page 126)

Preheat the oven to 350 degrees.

Using a sharp knife, make sixteen small incisions in the leg of lamb and slide the garlic halves into them. Make 12 small incisions between the fat and the flesh of the lamb and slide the anchovies into them. The anchovies should stay near the surface of the meat. Sprinkle with pepper.

Heat the duck fat over a high flame in a heavy ovenproof pan large enough to hold the entire leg of lamb. Quickly sear the lamb on all sides, then place the pan in the oven. Roast for $\frac{1}{2}$ hour, scatter the carrot, onion, and turnip around the roast and cook for another 20 minutes for medium rare, 30 minutes for medium, according to your preference.

Remove the meat from the oven and let rest in a warm place. Discard the fat from the pan, deglaze with the wine, and reduce by half over a high flame. Pass the sauce through a fine sieve, pushing on the vegetables to extract all the juices. Return the sauce to the saucepan just to heat it. Whisk in the anchovy butter, a few pieces at a time, until it is well incorporated. Slice the lamb and serve with the sauce on the side and with potatoes sautéed in duck fat. [*Yield: 6 servings*]

La Gasconnade de Jarret d'Agneau

LAMB SHANKS GASCON-STYLE

6 lamb shanks, about 1 pound
  each
Freshly ground black pepper to
  taste
2 tablespoons olive oil
3 carrots, minced
1 turnip, minced
4 onions, minced

1 leek, white part only, minced
12 anchovy fillets, packed in oil
$\frac{1}{4}$ cup tomato paste
14 garlic cloves, peeled
1 bottle dry red wine
3 ripe tomatoes, peeled, seeded,
  and halved

Preheat the oven to 300 degrees.

Season the shanks all over with pepper. Heat the olive oil in a large, heavy, ovenproof cast-iron pot over a high flame. Quickly sauté the shanks, turning them often to brown them on all sides. If the pot is too small to brown them at one time, do it in several batches. Return all the shanks to the pot and add the carrots, turnip, onions, and leek. Stir well and cook for 10 minutes, making sure the vegetables do not burn.

Add the anchovies, tomato paste, and four garlic cloves to the pot. Add the wine and bring to a boil. Cover and cook in the oven for $2\frac{1}{2}$ to 3 hours, or until the meat is very tender.

Blanch the remaining garlic cloves for 10 minutes in boiling water. Drain and set aside.

Remove the pot from the oven. Remove the shanks from the pot and place in a deep baking dish, large enough to hold the shanks in one layer. Place a tomato half on top of each shank and scatter the blanched garlic all over.

Pass the sauce through a fine sieve and pour over the meat. Return the shanks to the oven for 30 minutes. Serve with fresh pasta.   [*Yield: 6 servings*]

Rognons de Veau Entier Cuit en Cocotte

VEAL KIDNEYS WITH SHALLOTS AND GARLIC

3 very fresh veal kidneys
Salt and freshly ground pepper
   to taste
6 garlic cloves, peeled

7 shallots, peeled
12 tender leeks, white part only
1 cup port wine

Remove the first layer of fat from the kidneys and peel off the thin skin. The leftover fat should be very white. Trim the fat, leaving a thin layer. No meat should be exposed.

Heat a heavy enamel-covered cast-iron pot large enough to hold the kidneys comfortably in one layer, over a high flame. Sprinkle the kidneys with salt and pepper and add them to the pot. Sauté quickly until golden on both sides. Cover, lower the heat to medium, and cook for 10 minutes, turning them once in a while.

Meanwhile, blanch the garlic in lightly salted boiling water for 3 minutes and blanch six shallots for 5 minutes. Drain and set aside until ready to use.

Cook the leeks in lightly boiling water for 10 minutes. Drain and keep warm.

Remove the kidneys from the pot and keep warm.

Mince the remaining shallot. Discard the fat from the pot, then stir in the shallots. Cook for 5 minutes, or until lightly golden and soft. Deglaze the pot with the port wine and reduce by half. Thinly slice the kidneys and add them to the sauce along with their juices. Add the blanched garlic and shallots and cook for 1 minute, just to heat through. Divide the kidneys, shallots, and garlic among six warmed dinner plates and spoon some sauce over them. Garnish with the leeks and serve immediately.   [*Yield: 6 servings*]

Côte du Maître "Dou Maesté"

Salt and freshly ground black
pepper to taste
12 lamb shoulder chops, ½ inch
thick

¾ cup Roquefort butter (see recipe
page 178)

Lightly salt the chops and sprinkle them generously with pepper on both sides. Spread some Roquefort butter on one side of each chop. Stack two chops together, the buttered sides facing each other. Tie them together with some kitchen twine. You should have six stacks.

Preheat the oven to 500 degrees.

Over a high flame, heat a heavy, ovenproof frying pan, such as a cast-iron skillet, that is large enough to hold the chops without crowding. When the pan is hot, add the chops and cook for a few seconds, until they start to sizzle. Place the pan in the oven and cook for 8 to 10 minutes, according to taste. Remove the kitchen twine, being careful not to undo the stacks. Serve immediately.   [*Yield: 6 servings*]

Faux Filets au Roquefort et au Fruit Sec

STEAKS WITH ROQUEFORT-NUT SAUCE

2 top sirloin steaks, 1¾ pounds
  each
Salt and freshly ground black
  pepper to taste
2 tablespoons vegetable oil
4 tablespoons unsalted butter (½
  stick)
1 shallot, minced

½ cup Madeira wine
⅓ cup Roquefort butter (see recipe
  page 178), chilled
2 tablespoons coarsely chopped
  walnuts
1 tablespoon pine nuts
1 tablespoon almond slivers

Remove the steaks from the refrigerator 30 minutes before cooking. Season
with salt and pepper.

Heat the oil and 2 tablespoons of the butter in a large, heavy frying pan
over high heat. When the pan is very hot, add the steaks and cook for 4 to
5 minutes on each side. Remove them from the pan and keep warm until
ready to serve.

Discard the fat and add the minced shallot. Cook for 3 minutes, or until
golden. Deglaze the pan with the Madeira and reduce by half. Whisk in the
Roquefort butter, a few pieces at a time, until well incorporated.

Heat the remaining butter in a small frying pan, add the nuts, and sauté
over medium heat until they are lightly golden and warm. Cut each steak into
three serving pieces and place on six warmed dinner plates. Reserve the juice
that runs out and stir into the sauce. Spoon the sauce on the steaks and
sprinkle the warm nuts over them.   [*Yield: 6 servings*]

GAME

Lapin au Vin Vinaigré

RABBIT IN WINE AND VINEGAR SAUCE

1 small rabbit, about 3 pounds
Crushed white pepper to taste
Salt to taste
1 tablespoon herbes de Provence
  (see note page 95)

6 tablespoons vegetable oil
1 onion, minced
$\frac{2}{3}$ cup dry red wine
$\frac{1}{3}$ cup red wine vinegar
$\frac{3}{4}$ cup heavy cream

Have a butcher cut the rabbit into eight serving pieces: two shoulders, two back legs and four loins. Place the pieces in a bowl and sprinkle with the crushed white pepper, a little salt and the *herbes de Provence*. Rub 3 table-spoons of the oil all over the rabbit and marinate for 2 hours.

Heat the remaining oil in a large sauté pan over a high flame. Add the rabbit pieces: first the legs, then 2 minutes later the shoulders, and 2 minutes later the loins. Stir in the onion and sauté until the meat is golden brown, about 8 minutes. Cover, lower the heat to medium, and cook for 10 minutes. Be careful not to overcook the loins, or they will be dry. Remove from the pan and keep warm.

Degrease the pan, then deglaze it with the wine and vinegar. Reduce until the liquid is almost evaporated. Add the cream and reduce by a third. Season with salt. Return the meat to the pan and cook for 2 to 3 minutes to warm the pieces. Serve immediately with buttered noodles.   [*Yield: 3 servings*]

Civet de Lièvre à l'Armagnac

HARE IN ARMAGNAC

1 hare, about 4 pounds
¼ cup flour
Salt and freshly ground black
    pepper to taste
7 garlic cloves
6 tablespoons vegetable oil
⅓ pound prosciutto, chopped
3 tablespoons chopped parsley
3 shallots, chopped
1 cup Armagnac

2 cups full-bodied red wine
1 cup water
1 bouquet garni consisting of 1
    bay leaf, 1 teaspoon thyme, 10
    black peppercorns, and 8
    parsley sprigs
1 teaspoon quatre épices (see
    recipe page 175)
4 chicken livers
12 slices French baguette

Have a butcher cut the hare into eight serving pieces: two shoulders, two legs, and four loins. Combine the flour with salt and pepper. Mince six garlic cloves and set aside.

Heat 4 tablespoons of the oil over high heat in a heavy pot. Dredge the hare pieces in the seasoned flour and sauté until golden brown on all sides. Add the prosciutto, parsley, minced garlic, and shallots, and stir well. Add ⅔ cup of the Armagnac and flambé until the flames disappear. Be careful because Armagnac can create high flames. When the flames die down, add the wine, water, bouquet garni, and *quatre épices.* Lower the heat to medium, cover, and cook for 1¼ hours to 1½ hours, or until the meat is tender.

Remove the meat from the pot and keep warm. Reduce the cooking liquid to 2 cups over high heat. Turn off the heat. Meanwhile, cut the bread slices in half and heat the remaining 2 tablespoons oil in a small frying pan. Fry the bread slices over medium heat until they are golden on both sides. Drain them on paper towels and rub both sides with the remaining garlic clove. Keep warm until ready to serve.

Place the chicken livers and the remaining Armagnac in the bowl of a food processor and puree to a smooth consistency. Pour the mixture into a mixing bowl.

Stirring constantly, slowly add about 1 cup of cooking liquid to the liver mixture, making sure it does not curdle. Stir the mixture back into the pot to thicken the cooking liquid, add the hare, and mix. Serve immediately with the garlic croutons.   [*Yield: 6 servings*]

Petit Steak de Venaison aux Airelles

VENISON STEAKS WITH CRANBERRIES

1 cup fresh cranberries
$\frac{1}{4}$ cup port wine
2 cups dry red wine
1 cup red wine vinegar
1 onion, sliced
2 carrots, sliced
2 teaspoons herbes de Provence
  (see note page 95)
1 cup Armagnac
2 pounds boned venison fillet
Salt and freshly ground black
  pepper to taste
3 garlic cloves
3 tablespoons rendered duck fat
  (see recipe page 176)
$\frac{1}{4}$ cup heavy cream

Combine the cranberries and the port in a small saucepan. Bring to a simmer over medium heat and cook for 3 minutes, or until the cranberries start to soften. Remove from the heat and set aside.

Combine the wine, vinegar, onion, carrots, *herbes de Provence,* and half of the Armagnac. Sprinkle the fillet with salt and pepper. Peel the garlic cloves, cut them lengthwise, and rub the meat all over with them. Place the meat in the marinade and let it sit at room temperature for 3 hours.

Remove the meat from the marinade and dry it thoroughly with paper towels. Set the marinade aside. Cut the fillet into 1-inch-thick medallions. Drain the cranberries and reserve the port.

Heat the duck fat over high heat in a heavy frying pan. Quickly sauté the meat, about 3 minutes on each side. Remove the steaks from the pan and keep warm.

Discard the fat from the pan. Add half of the cranberries and sauté quickly. Add the marinade and the reserved port. Bring to a boil and cook for 10 minutes. Strain the sauce through a fine sieve and return it to the pan.

Bring the sauce back to a boil, add the cream and the remaining Armagnac, and boil until the sauce thickens slightly. Stir in the juices from the meat, along with the remaining cranberries. Place the venison steaks on a warmed serving platter, spoon the sauce over them, and serve immediately. [*Yield: 6 servings*]

Game

One of the most heated battles among culinary experts centers on the preparation of game. Traditionally, game is hung and aged, a process known as *faisandé*. Many hunters and/or cooks insist on this process; they insist that otherwise the meat will be heavy, unsavory, or even toxic.

According to Daguin, game, especially birds, are better fresh—a day or two after they are killed. If the meat appears to be tough, a long, slow cooking will tenderize it.

Faisan en Marinade

MARINATED PHEASANT

3 pheasants, about 2½ pounds
  each
3 cups dry red wine
1 small onion, thinly sliced
1 small carrot, thinly sliced
1 garlic clove, crushed
½ cup red wine vinegar
¾ cup Armagnac
2 tablespoons herbes de Provence
  (see note page 95)

1½ cups vegetable oil
10 black peppercorns
¼ cup flour
Salt and freshly ground black
  pepper to taste
2 pounds Brussels sprouts
¼ cup heavy cream

The day before serving the pheasant, remove the legs and the breasts from the carcasses with a sharp boning knife. Using a small paring knife, debone the thigh. Begin by running the tip of the blade around the exposed bone at the thigh joint to separate the meat from the bone. Next, work the blade around the bone and push the meat toward the leg joint. Slice through the joint between the leg and the thigh. Repeat with the other leg.

In a large mixing bowl, combine the red wine, onion, carrot, garlic, vinegar, Armagnac, and 1 tablespoon of the *herbes de Provence*. Add the pheasant legs, coat them well with the mixture, cover, and marinate them in the refrigerator overnight.

In another mixing bowl, combine the oil, the remaining *herbes de Provence*, and the peppercorns. Add the breasts, coat them well with the mixture, cover, and marinate them in the refrigerator overnight.

The next day, remove the legs from the marinade and dry them thoroughly with paper towels. Dredge them in the flour and shake off the excess. Remove ¼ cup of oil from the breasts' marinade and heat it in a heavy pot over a medium-high flame. Sauté the legs for 10 minutes, or until they are golden brown on all sides. Discard the excess oil and pour the red wine marinade into the pot. Bring to a boil, season with salt and pepper, and simmer, covered, for 45 minutes to 1 hour, until the legs are tender. The cooking time will depend on the quality of the pheasants.

Meanwhile, blanch the Brussels sprouts in lightly salted water for 15 minutes. Drain and plunge them into ice water. Drain again and set aside until ready to use.

Remove the legs from the pot and place on a warmed serving platter. Keep warm. Pass the sauce through a fine sieve and return the liquid to the pot. Reduce the sauce over high heat for about 10 minutes or to $1\frac{1}{4}$ cups. Add the cream to the pot and reduce over high heat for 2 minutes or until the sauce thickens slightly. Adjust the seasoning with salt and pepper. Meanwhile, remove the breasts from the marinade and dry lightly with a paper towel. Sprinkle them with salt and pepper. Heat 3 tablespoons of the oil from the marinade over high flame in a large frying pan. Sauté the breasts for 4 to 5 minutes on each side according to taste.

In another frying pan heat 4 tablespoons of the oil from the marinade and sauté the Brussels sprouts briefly, just to heat them through.

Arrange the pheasant legs and breasts on a warmed serving platter and spoon the sauce over them. Serve immediately with the sprouts on the side. [*Yield: 10 servings*]

STEWS

Cassoulet Toulousain

CASSOULET TOULOUSAIN

2 pounds dried beans, such as navy or Great Northern
7 ounces fresh pork rind
10 ounces fresh slab bacon
1 carrot, peeled
3 onions, peeled
5 cloves
2 bouquets garnis, each consisting of $\frac{3}{4}$ teaspoon thyme, 1 bay leaf, 5 sprigs parsley, and 10 black peppercorns
12 garlic cloves, peeled
Salt to taste
$\frac{1}{2}$ cup fat from the duck confit
2 pounds lamb shanks, boned and cut into 2- by 2-inch cubes

2 pounds pork shoulder, boned and cut into 2- by 2-inch cubes
Freshly ground black pepper to taste
3 tomatoes, peeled and seeded
2 quarts good rich duck or chicken stock (see recipe page 173)
$\frac{1}{2}$ pound garlic sausage
4 duck legs confit (see page 46)
$\frac{3}{4}$ pound fresh pork sausage (do not use sweet or spicy sausage)
$\frac{3}{4}$ cup fresh bread crumbs

Two days before serving the cassoulet, soak the beans in water overnight.

The next day, drain the beans and place them in a large pot. Add the pork rind, fresh bacon, carrot, one onion pierced with the five cloves, one bouquet garni, and six cloves of garlic. Season with a little salt and cover with water. Bring to a boil and simmer for 30 to 40 minutes, or until the beans are almost cooked. Drain.

Heat 3 tablespoons of the duck fat in a large frying pan, add the lamb, and sauté over medium-high heat until well browned on all sides. Remove from the pan. Repeat with the pork. Season with salt and pepper. Chop the remaining onions and crush the remaining garlic. Remove and discard from the beans the bouquet garni, onion, and carrot. Cut the bacon into 1-inch cubes.

In a large, heavy pot, place the sautéed meats along with the chopped onions, crushed garlic, the remaining bouquet garni, and the tomatoes. Lightly season with salt, cover with 1 quart of the stock, and simmer for $1\frac{1}{2}$ hours.

When the meats are cooked, add the beans, pork rind, garlic, and bacon to the pot along with the garlic sausage and the *confit*. The mixture should

be moist and soupy. If necessary, add more stock, taste, and adjust the seasonings, and simmer for $\frac{1}{2}$ hour. Sauté the fresh sausage in a frying pan until it is golden brown on all sides.

Remove the meats, except the bacon, from the pot and discard the pork rind. Cut the garlic sausage into $\frac{1}{2}$-inch-thick slices. Cut the duck legs in half and slice the fresh sausage into 2-inch pieces. In a large earthenware casserole or an enamel-coated, cast-iron ovenproof pot, spread half of the beans at the bottom, arrange the lamb, and pork shoulder on top. Cover with the remaining beans and then layer the duck *confit,* the garlic sausage, and the sausage on top. Pour the remaining broth over the meats and the beans. Cover and refrigerate overnight.

The day you serve the cassoulet, remove it from the refrigerator 3 hours before cooking to bring it to room temperature.

Preheat the oven to 300 degrees.

Heat the remaining 5 tablespoons duck fat. Sprinkle bread crumbs, to cover, over the cassoulet, then pour the hot duck fat all over it. Place the casserole in a deep pan filled with hot water and bake for 2 hours, or until the cassoulet is very hot. If the cassoulet seems to become too dry during the cooking, add a little broth or water to the pot. Serve immediately.   [*Yield: 12 to 15 servings*]

Anatole France on Cassoulet

I am going to lead you to a little tavern on the rue Vavin, chez Clemence, which makes only one dish, but what a superb dish it is! . . . To be good, it must have cooked very slowly for a long time. Clemence's cassoulet has been cooking for twenty years. She replenishes the pot sometimes with goose, sometimes with pork fat, sometimes she puts in a sausage or some haricot beans, but it is always the same cassoulet. The basis remains and this ancient and precious substance gives it the savor one finds in the paintings of the old Venetian masters, in the amber flesh tints of their women. Come, I want you to taste Clemence's cassoulet."

Anatole France—*Histoire Comique*

Blanquette de Veau au Gingembre

VEAL STEW WITH GINGER

3 pounds veal stew meat, boned
   and cut into 3-inch cubes
Salt and freshly ground white
   pepper to taste
1 teaspoon thyme
1 bay leaf
2 leeks, chopped
1 onion, chopped
1 celery stalk, chopped

2 garlic cloves, chopped
1 cup dry white wine
2 tablespoons unsalted butter
1 shallot, minced
3 tablespoons flour
¾ cup cream
1 ounce fresh ginger, peeled and
   cut into very fine julienne

The day before you plan to make the stew, place the meat in a large pot. Cover with cold water and season with salt, pepper, thyme, and a bay leaf. Let it stand at room temperature for 1 hour. Bring the liquid to a boil over medium-high heat. Boil for 5 minutes, skimming often. Drain and rinse the meat under cold water. Wrap the veal in a damp towel and refrigerate until ready to use.

When ready to cook, place the meat in a nonaluminum pot along with the leeks, onion, celery, and garlic. Add the white wine and cover with about 4 cups water. Season lightly with salt and pepper. Bring to a low simmer and cook, partly covered, for 2 hours, or until the meat is tender and can easily be pierced with a skewer.

Remove the meat from the pot and keep warm by adding a ladle of hot broth. Pass the remaining broth through a fine sieve, return to the pot, and reduce to about 2½ cups. Meanwhile, melt the butter in a saucepan over low heat. Add the shallot and cook for 5 minutes, making sure that the shallot does not brown. Add the flour to the pan and cook, stirring constantly, for 4 minutes. Remove the pan from the heat and add the hot broth, all at once, stirring constantly. Return the pan to the heat and stir in the cream. Cook for 10 minutes, stirring constantly, then taste, and adjust the seasoning. Add the meat to the pan along with the julienned ginger and cook a few minutes to heat the meat through. Serve with broiled rice, glazed pearl onions, and sautéed mushrooms.   [*Yield: 6 servings*]

Blanquette

Blanquette is a white râgout, long a standard in French bour-
geois cooking—as important and ubiquitous as *boeuf bourguignon*
or *coq au vin*. Traditionally prepared with veal, a *blanquette* can
be quite successfully paired with any white meat, such as spring
lamb, chicken, or turkey.

The beauty of a *blanquette* is in its pristine milk-white color.
The meat is first blanched, then simmered in a white court bouillon and, at last, the sauce is thickened with a white roux and
enriched with cream. The classic garnish is generally made of
white pearl onions and button mushrooms. In order to insure the
whiteness of your *blanquette,* here are several don'ts:

—Don't use an aluminum pot; it can turn the stew a murky,
unappetizing gray.

—Don't allow the broth to boil; this will make the liquid cloudy.
Simmer it instead.

—Don't include a lot of vegetables with high carotene content,
such as carrots or beets; their coloring will seep into the sauce.

—Don't allow the roux to darken. Cook it, over low heat, long
enough to achieve the proper consistency, then add the liquid
before it turns golden.

—Don't use grilled onions for the broth.

Blanquette d'Agneau

LAMB STEW, BLANQUETTE STYLE

6 lamb shanks, about one pound
   each, boned
Salt and freshly ground white
   pepper to taste
2 teaspoons herbes de Provence
   (see note page 95)
3 lemons
2 leeks, chopped
1 celery stalk, chopped

1 onion, chopped
2 garlic cloves, chopped
1 pound celeriac, peeled
1 cup dry white wine
5 tablespoons unsalted butter
1 shallot, minced
2 tablespoons flour
$\frac{3}{4}$ cup heavy cream
2 tablespoons chopped parsley

The day before serving the *blanquette,* cut the meat into 1-inch cubes and place them with the salt, pepper, and herbs in a large pot. Cover with cold water and let stand at room temperature for 1 hour. Bring the water to a boil over medium-high heat. Boil for 5 minutes, skimming often. Drain and rinse the meat under cold water. Wrap the meat in a damp cloth and refrigerate until ready to use.

When ready to cook, rub the meat all over with two of the lemons and place it in a nonaluminum pot. Add the leeks, celery, onion, garlic, and celeriac. Add the wine and cover with about 4 cups water. Lightly season with salt and pepper. Slowly bring to a simmer and cook, partly covered, for $1\frac{1}{2}$ hours, or until the meat is tender. After 1 hour remove the celeriac from the pot and set it aside.

Remove the meat from the pot and keep it warm by adding a ladle of warm broth. This will prevent the meat from drying out. Pass the remaining broth through a fine sieve, return to the pot, and reduce it to $2\frac{1}{2}$ cups. Meanwhile, melt 2 tablespoons of the butter in a saucepan over low heat. Add the shallot and cook for 5 minutes, or until soft. Add the flour and cook, stirring, for 4 minutes. Remove the pan from the heat and add the hot broth, all at once, stirring constantly. Return the pan to the heat and stir in the cream. Cook for 10 minutes, stirring constantly, then taste and adjust the salt and pepper. Stir in the juice of the remaining lemon. Add the meat to the pan to heat it through. Meanwhile, cut the celeriac into $\frac{1}{2}$-inch slices and sauté in the remaining butter until lightly golden.

To serve, place the stew in a serving dish, sprinkle with parsley, and serve the celeriac slices on the side. Rice is a good accompaniment to this dish. [*Yield: 6 servings*]

Blanquette de Dinde

TURKEY STEW, BLANQUETTE STYLE

3½-pound boneless turkey breast,
   cut into 1-inch cubes
Salt and freshly ground white
   pepper to taste
2 teaspoons herbes de Provence
   (see note page 95)
2 leeks, chopped
1 onion, chopped
2 garlic cloves, chopped
1 cup dry white wine

2 cups water
4 tablespoons unsalted butter (½
   stick)
1 shallot, minced
2 tablespoons flour
½ cup heavy cream
3 tablespoons olive oil
3 tomatoes, peeled, halved and
   seeded

The day before you serve the *blanquette,* place the turkey in a large pot, cover with cold water, and season with salt, pepper, and the *herbes de Provence.* Let stand at room temperature for 1 hour. Bring the water to a boil over medium-high heat and cook for 5 minutes, skimming frequently. Drain and rinse the meat under cold running water. Wrap the meat in a damp cloth and refrigerate until ready to use. When ready to cook, place the meat in a large pot, add the leeks, onion, and garlic. Add the wine and cover with the water. Lightly season with salt and pepper. Slowly bring to a simmer and cook, covered, for 45 minutes to 1 hour, or until the meat is tender but not dry.

Remove the meat from the pot and keep warm with a ladle of hot broth. Pass the broth through a fine sieve. You should have about 2½ cups, reduce if necessary. Melt the butter in a small saucepan, add the shallot, and cook over low heat for 5 minutes, or until soft. Add the flour and cook, stirring, for 4 minutes. Remove the pan from the heat and add the hot broth, all at once, stirring constantly. Return the saucepan to the heat and stir in the cream. Cook for 10 minutes, stirring constantly. Season with salt and pepper. Return the meat to the sauce to heat it through.

Meanwhile, heat the olive oil in a large frying pan, add the tomatoes, season with salt and pepper, and cook, covered, for 10 minutes. Serve the blanquette hot, with the tomatoes on the side.   [*Yield: 6 servings*]

Daube de Boeuf Gasconne

BEEF STEW GASCON STYLE

3 pounds beef shin, boned and
cut into 2-inch cubes
3 pounds beef shoulder meat,
boned and cut into 2-inch
cubes
3 pounds brisket, cut into 2-inch
cubes
5 carrots
6 onions
2 garlic heads plus 6 cloves
2 quarts dry red wine
1 tablespoon quatre épices (see
recipe page 175)
12 black peppercorns

3 leeks, trimmed
4 celery stalks
1 calf's foot, blanched
1 small ham bone
1 fresh pig knuckle
¾ cup vegetable oil
1 cup Armagnac
1 cup water
1 bouquet garni consisting of 1
teaspoon thyme, 2 bay leaves,
6 sprigs parsley, and 10 black
peppercorns
Salt to taste
12 small potatoes, peeled

The day before you serve the stew, place the meats in a noncorrosive pot. Mince two carrots and two onions. Peel the two garlic heads and cut the cloves crosswise; add them to the pot. Cover with the wine and stir in the *quatre épices* and the peppercorns. Cover and let marinate in the refrigerator.

The next day, preheat the oven to 300 degrees.

Finely mince the remaining carrots, onions, and garlic, the leeks, and celery. Remove the meats from the marinade and drain well. Strain and reserve the marinade. Place the calf's foot, the ham bone, and the pig knuckle at the bottom of a heavy pot, such as cast iron, large enough to hold the meats and the vegetables.

Using a heavy frying pan, heat 3 tablespoons of the oil and sauté a quarter of the meat over high heat until the meat is well browned on all sides. Remove with a slotted spoon and place in the heavy pot. Repeat with remaining meat. Place half the vegetables into the pan, cover, and sweat them over medium heat for 10 minutes. Do not brown the vegetables. Add them to the pot. Repeat with remaining vegetables. Deglaze the pan with the marinade, bring to a boil, and pour it into the pot. Add the Armagnac, water,

and the bouquet garni. Season with salt, cover, and cook in the oven for 3 hours, or until the meats are tender. This can be done a day or two before serving. When ready to serve, remove the bones and the calf's foot, and heat the stew over medium flame, add the potatoes, and cook for 40 minutes. Serve hot.   [*Yield: 10 to 12 servings*]

Daube d'Agneau aux Gousses d'Ail

LAMB STEW WITH GARLIC CLOVES

6½ pounds lamb stew meats, a
    combination of shank,
    shoulder, and breast
2 tablespoons rendered duck fat
    (see recipe page 176)
20 pearl onions, peeled
20 garlic cloves, peeled
2 tablespoons tomato paste

1 teaspoon thyme
½ teaspoon rosemary
½ teaspoon savory
1 bay leaf
Salt and freshly ground black
    pepper to taste
2 cups flour
12 small new potatoes, peeled

Preheat the oven to 225 degrees.

Bone and remove any fat from the shanks and the shoulder. Cut the meat into 2-inch cubes. Trim off as much fat as possible from the breast and cut into 2-inch pieces.

In a cast-iron pot, heat the duck fat over high heat. Add a few pieces of meat at a time and sauté until they are golden brown on all sides. Remove the meat from the pot with a slotted spoon and repeat with the remaining pieces. Discard the fat from the pot. Return the meat to the pot, add the onions, garlic, and tomato paste, and cook over medium heat for 15 minutes, stirring occasionally. Add some water to the pot to just cover the meat, season with the thyme, rosemary, savory, bay leaf, salt, and pepper, and bring to a boil. Cover and remove from the heat.

Combine the flour with about 1¼ cups of water in a mixing bowl to form a dough. Press the dough all around the edges of the lid to form a seal, and bake for 7 hours. Remove the pot from the oven and break the seal. Carefully spoon out the fat from the stew. Add the potatoes to the pot and cook over medium heat for 20 minutes, or until they are tender. Serve hot.   [*Yield: 6 servings*]

Noix de Cuisse de Boeuf Braisée Bourgeoise

BRAISED BEEF WITH VEGETABLES

3 garlic heads
1 piece top round, about 3 pounds
Salt and freshly ground black pepper to taste
6 carrots, peeled
4 onions, peeled
8 tomatoes
3 tablespoons vegetable oil

3 tablespoons tomato paste
3 tablespoons strong Dijon-style mustard
2 tablespoons flour
1 bottle Zinfandel or robust other red wine
3 celery stalks
6 small new potatoes, peeled

The day before you plan to serve the stew, peel one head of garlic, split the cloves in half, and remove any green sprout. Using a small knife, make deep incisions in the meat and insert the garlic halves into them. Sprinkle with salt and pepper, and refrigerate, covered, overnight. Bring the meat to room temperature 1 hour before cooking.

When ready to cook, preheat the oven to 300 degrees.

Chop four carrots and the onions, and peel, seed, and chop the tomatoes.

Heat the oil in a heavy pot large enough to hold the meat and the vegetables. Brown the meat on all sides over medium-high heat. Add the tomato paste, mustard, and flour, lower the heat, and cook for 5 minutes. Remove the meat from the pot, add the carrots, tomatoes, and onions, and sauté for 10 minutes, or until the carrots and onions soften. Return the meat to the pot, add the wine, then add enough water to cover the meat. Bake, covered, for 3 hours, or until the meat is very tender and a fork goes in easily. Remove the pot from the oven and pass the sauce through a fine sieve.

Cut the celery and the remaining carrots into thick sticks. Return the sauce to the pot along with the meat and the potatoes. Simmer for 30 minutes. Ten minutes before the end of the cooking time, add the carrots and the celery sticks. Serve hot.   [*Yield: 6 servings*]

Daube de Boeuf à l'Armagnac

DAUBE OF BEEF IN ARMAGNAC

This stew is best when made two or three days before serving.

6 tablespoons vegetable oil
3 pounds beef shin, cut into
   3-inch cubes
6 tablespoons flour
¾ cup plus 2 tablespoons
   Armagnac
2 tablespoons unsalted butter
½ pound prosciutto, finely
   chopped
5 garlic cloves, finely chopped

1 large onion, finely chopped
3 medium carrots, finely chopped
1 bottle full-bodied red wine
1 quart water
1 bouquet garni consisting of 5
   sprigs parsley, 1 bay leaf, and
   1 teaspoon dried thyme
Salt and freshly ground black
   pepper to taste
6 slices good quality white bread

In a large frying pan, heat 3 tablespoons of oil over a high flame and sauté the meat until brown on all sides. Sprinkle the flour over the meat and cook for a few minutes, until the flour starts to brown.

Transfer the meat to a heavy casserole, such as a cast-iron pot. Pour ¾ cup Armagnac over it and flambé until the flames disappear. Be careful because Armagnac can create high flames. Meanwhile, heat the butter in a frying pan and sauté the prosciutto, garlic, onion, and carrots over high heat for 5 minutes, or until golden. Add to the meat in the casserole and stir well. Add the wine, water, the bouquet garni, salt, and pepper. Bring to a boil, lower the heat to a very low simmer, and cook, covered, for 6 hours. Remove from the flame and cool at room temperature. Refrigerate until ready to serve.

When ready to serve, bring the stew slowly to a boil, over medium heat.

Cut each bread slice diagonally to form two triangles. Heat the remaining oil in a small frying pan over medium heat and sauté the bread for 2 minutes on each side or until golden. Keep warm until ready to serve.

Just before serving, stir the 2 tablespoons of Armagnac into the hot stew and serve immediately with the fried bread triangles.   [*Yield: 6 servings*]

SAUCES

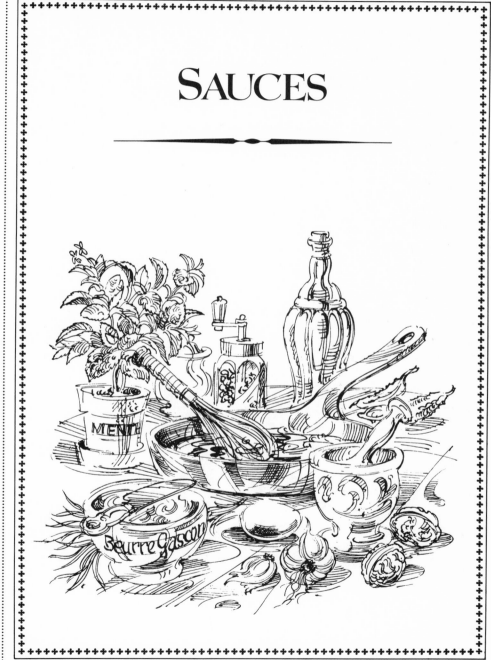

Beurre Gascon

GASCON BUTTER

This "butter" is usually served at the Hôtel de France with an aperitif. It makes a very tasty spread for country-style French bread.

1 cup full-bodied red wine
2 shallots, minced
¾ cup rendered duck fat, chilled
   (see recipe page 176)

Salt and freshly ground black
   pepper to taste

Reduce the wine with the shallots in a small saucepan over medium heat until the liquid is almost evaporated. Remove the pan from the heat.

Slowly whisk in the duck fat, a few pieces at a time, to form an emulsion. The result should be creamy. Season with salt and pepper, and cool in the refrigerator, stirring every 30 minutes to keep the shallots from falling to the bottom, until the fat is set. The butter will keep in the refrigerator, in a sealed container, for several weeks.   [*Yield: ¾ cup*]

Sauce Auscitaine

AUSCITAINE SAUCE

This is a béarnaise sauce made with duck fat. The fat gives it a rich, intense flavor. It is the perfect accompaniment for grilled meats, especially magret.

3 shallots, minced
1 tablespoon minced tarragon
12 mint leaves, minced
½ cup red wine vinegar
1 tablespoon red wine

Salt to taste
6 white peppercorns, crushed
3 eggs yolks
1 cup rendered duck fat, warmed
(see recipe page 176)

In a heavy-gauge copper saucepan, combine the shallots, tarragon, mint, red wine vinegar, wine, salt, and pepper. Bring the mixture to a boil and reduce by three-fourths. Remove from the heat and cool.

When the wine mixture is lukewarm, whisk in the egg yolks and return the saucepan to the stove over very low heat. Whisk constantly, making sure the eggs do not curdle. When the mixture is foamy and starts to thicken, add the duck fat in a thin stream, whisking constantly. The mixture should form a smooth, thick emulsion. This sauce can be kept warm in a *bain-marie* for 1 hour until ready to serve.   [*Yield: 1½ cups*]

Sauce à l'Ail et aux Noix

WALNUT AND GARLIC SAUCE

In Gascony, we revere garlic as much as do the natives of Provence. We usually use the whole clove, peeled or not, cooked thoroughly until soft. In this recipe, the garlic is more of a condiment. For best results, mash it with a mortar and pestle rather than a blender or food processor. Serve with grilled meats.

5 garlic cloves, peeled
12 walnuts, shelled
1 tablespoon white wine vinegar
Salt and freshly ground black
   pepper to taste

$\frac{2}{3}$ cup vegetable oil
2 teaspoons minced fresh chervil
1 teaspoon minced fresh
   marjoram

In a mortar, combine the garlic, walnuts, and white wine vinegar. Pound, using a pestle, until well combined and the mixture forms a paste. Season with salt and pepper, and slowly add the oil to form an emulsion, as you would for a mayonnaise. Fold in the minced herbs and let stand at room temperature until ready to serve.   [*Yield: $\frac{3}{4}$ cup*]

La Sauce Gribiche

CAPERS AND CORNICHONS SAUCE

This is picante sauce to serve with a *poule au pot*.

2 hard-cooked eggs
1 tablespoon Dijon-style mustard
Salt and freshly ground black
    pepper to taste
1 cup vegetable oil
2 tablespoons red wine vinegar
5 cornichons, finely chopped

2 tablespoons capers, finely
    chopped
1 tablespoon chopped parsley
1 tablespoon chopped fresh chervil
2 teaspoons chopped fresh
    tarragon

Peel the eggs and separate the yolks from the whites. Small dice whites and reserve until ready to use.

Place the yolks into a mixing bowl and mash them with a fork or the back of a spoon to form a smooth paste. Stir in the mustard and season with salt and pepper.

Stirring constantly, add the oil, a few drops at a time, to make an emulsion, as you would for a mayonnaise. When all the oil is incorporated, stir in the vinegar, cornichons, capers, all the herbs and the reserved egg whites. Taste and adjust the seasoning. Refrigerate until ready to serve.   [*Yield: 1½ cups*]

DESSERTS

Pastis Gascon

FLAKY APPLE PIE

This fragrant, flaky pie, redolent of orange flower water and Armagnac, is among the most typical of Gascon desserts.

It is labor intensive but rewarding. The traditional dough, with a phyllo-like texture, is a mixture of flour, water, and eggs worked to a consistency of bread dough and stretched, on floured bed sheets, to a very thin layer.

The recipe below has been adapted for commercial phyllo dough.

3 medium-size Granny Smith apples, peeled, cored, and thinly sliced
$\frac{1}{4}$ cup Armagnac
4 tablespoons unsalted butter ($\frac{1}{2}$ stick)

1 tablespoon orange flower water
10 sheets phyllo pastry, thawed
3 tablespoons sugar

The day before you plan to serve the *pastis,* marinate the apples in 3 tablespoons of Armagnac.

When ready to prepare the *pastis,* melt the butter in a small saucepan over medium heat. Stir in 1 teaspoon of the orange water and 1 tablespoon of the Armagnac. Set aside until ready to use.

Preheat the oven to 300 degrees.

Place the phyllo pastry on a work surface and cover it with a damp cloth to keep it moist. Using a small pastry brush, grease the bottom and the sides of a 10-inch glass pie plate with the butter mixture. Drape one phyllo sheet over the bottom of the plate, with the edges hanging over the plate rim evenly. Brush with the butter mixture. Lay over another phyllo sheet and butter the entire surface generously—make sure you butter the corners so they do not dry out. Repeat with the remaining sheets, saving two sheets to cover the top. Always keep the phyllo covered with the damp cloth or it will dry out.

Pour the apples and Armagnac into the dish. Sprinkle with the sugar and the remaining 2 teaspoons orange water. Fold the hanging edges of the pastry over the apples. Fold the remaining two sheets of phyllo in half, butter them

well on both sides, and place them over the apples. Tuck the overlap into the sides of the pie. Brush with the remaining butter.

Bake for 40 to 45 minutes, or until the inside is bubbly and the top lightly golden. Serve warm.   [*Yield: 8 servings*]

ORANGE FLOWER WATER: a water distilled from orange flowers. It is available in specialty or gourmet shops. The best kind comes from Provence, France.

Cheeses

The hilly lands of Armagnac, rising to the mountains of the Bearn and the Basque country, are well suited to sheep and goat farming. Many, if not most, of the traditional Gascon cheeses are produced from ewe's or goat's milk.

The following is a representative (but by no means exhaustive) survey of cheeses you might find on a Gascon table.

BETHMALE is a cow's cheese produced in the southeastern part of the region. It is a winter cheese, given a longer aging period to become hard and suitable for grating.

CHÈVRE FRAIS is, of course, a goat cheese, light and mild. Gascons will often add a pinch of sugar and a dash of Armagnac to the cheese, whip it, and serve it as a spread.

FROMAGE DES PYRENÉES is a mild sheep cheese produced in various parts of the Pyrenees mountains. They all vary slightly in texture and sharpness depending on their processing and aging. Among the most reputable ones is the FROMAGE DE LARUNS.

POUSTAGNACQ is a sheep's milk cheese from the Landes. It is a jar-fermented, soft cheese with a semimild taste.

ROCAMADOUR or CABECOU DE ROCAMADOUR is either a goat or sheep cheese with a nutty flavor, produced from late spring to autumn, in a thin disc. The sheep cheese is tender; the goat variety is firm.

Glace aux Pruneaux

PRUNE ICE CREAM

2½ cups prunes, pitted
1 cup Armagnac
1 quart milk

1 cup sugar
8 egg yolks

Ten days before you plan to serve the ice cream, combine the prunes and the Armagnac in a covered container. Set in a cool place.

When you are ready to make the ice cream, remove six prunes from the container and set aside. Place the remaining prunes and the Armagnac in the bowl of a food processor and process to a coarse purée. Set aside until ready to use. In a saucepan, combine the milk with two thirds of the sugar. Bring the mixture just to a boil over medium heat. Remove from the heat.

Meanwhile, beat the remaining sugar with the yolks until the mixture is pale yellow and thick. Slowly combine 1 cup of the hot milk with the yolks, stirring constantly. Pour the egg mixture into the saucepan and cook, stirring constantly, over medium heat until the temperature reaches 175 degrees on a candy thermometer and the mixture coats the back of a spoon. Immediately remove the saucepan from the heat and let cool.

When the mixture is completely cool, stir in the prune purée and pour the mixture into the bowl of an ice cream maker. Freeze according to the manufacturer's instructions.

To serve, scoop some ice cream into serving dishes and garnish with the reserved prunes.   [*Yield: 1¼ quarts*]

Confiture de Vieux Garçon

The origins of Confiture de Vieux Garçon are lost in the haze of the distant past. It is a very ancient, traditional recipe, but while its precise derivation is not known, its purpose is simply explained. Confiture de Vieux Garçon, translates literally as "jam of the old boy"—referring to the fact that it was made by unmarried gentlemen, who perhaps might not have known all the fine points of haute cuisine, but knew enough to put fresh berries in a jar and pour some Armagnac over them.

This delicious concoction is traditionally made of a mixture of red berries (in no particular quantities), such as raspberries, strawberries, boysenberries, and black currants. All that is required is a tall jar and a bottle of Armagnac. Each kind of berry is added to the jar during its harvest season. For example, rinse and dry some strawberries, then place them in the jar. Cover them with Armagnac.

When the raspberry season comes around, add some to the jar, making sure they are covered with enough Armagnac. Continue adding berries throughout the summer. By the end of the season, the jar should be filled and put aside for two to three month before eating. It will keep for up to a year. If the level of Armagnac goes down, simply add some more to completely cover the fruit. Confiture de Vieux Garçon makes a delightful after-dinner cordial. Spoon some of the fruit into a brandy glass and pour some of the liqueur over it.

Pruneaux au Vin Rouge Épicé et aux Zestes d'Oranges

PRUNES IN SPICED RED WINE WITH ORANGE ZESTS

This delicious and unusual dessert can be served as is, but is also terrific over a scoop of vanilla ice cream.

1 bottle Merlot or quality red wine
1 cup sugar
3 tablespoons whole black peppercorns, wrapped in cheesecloth

1 tablespoon freshly ground black peppercorns
2 oranges
2 pounds prunes, pitted

At least 24 hours before serving, combine the wine, sugar, whole peppercorns and ground peppercorns in a large glass bowl.

Rinse and dry the oranges. Remove the zest from the oranges and add to the wine. Squeeze the oranges and strain the juice into the wine mixture. Add the prunes to the bowl and stir to coat them well. Marinate for at least 24 hours in the refrigerator. To serve, remove the orange zests and the peppercorns in cheesecloth. Serve cool.   [*Yield: 12 servings*]

Tarte aux Pruneaux

PRUNE TART

PÂTE BRISÉE:

1½ cups all-purpose flour

A pinch of salt

12 tablespoons unsalted butter
  (1½ sticks), at room
  temperature

2 to 3 tablespoons water

FILLING:

3 cups prunes, pitted

Juice of half a lemon

12 tablespoons unsalted butter
  (1½ sticks), at room
  temperature

1 cup confectioners' sugar

3 medium eggs

¼ cup flour

1½ cups almonds, finely ground

¼ cup Armagnac

⅓ cup apricot preserves, warmed

To make the crust: In a mixing bowl, combine the flour with the salt. Cut the butter into small cubes and add to the bowl. Mix it with the flour, using the tips of your fingers, until the mixture resembles coarse meal. Add the water, a tablespoon at a time, to form a soft dough. Use only as much water as needed to form the dough. On a lightly floured work surface roll out the dough into a circle to fit a 10½-inch tart mold. Lay the dough over the mold and gently press it against the bottom and the sides with your fingers. Trim excess dough. Refrigerate for 1 hour, or until ready to use.

To make the filling: Place the prunes in a bowl and cover with hot water. Stir in the lemon juice and set aside for 30 minutes, or until they are plumped. Drain and set aside until ready to use.

Preheat the oven to 400 degrees.

In a large mixing bowl, combine the butter and sugar, and beat until the mixture becomes light in color and fluffy. Add the eggs, one at a time, beating well after each addition. Fold in the flour and the ground almonds.

Pour this mixture into the prepared mold, smooth it out with a spatula, and arrange the prunes on top. Bake for 30 to 35 minutes, or until the surface turns golden brown. Remove the tart from the oven and pour over the Armagnac. Cool for a few minutes, then brush the top with the warm apricot preserves to glaze. Serve at room temperature.   [*Yield: 8 to 10 servings*]

Henri IV and Lavarenne

Henri IV had a decidedly sweet tooth. He made certain that his pockets were amply supplied with bonbons, which he passed out at court to placate the gentlemen and persuade the ladies. These candies were first made when the crusaders returned with sugar from the East.

Henri IV loved to develop talent in his kitchens and spotted one raw recruit, a kitchen boy named Lavarenne, in the household of his sister the Dutchess du Bars.

Lavarenne, aside from handling the king's *billets doux* to his mistresses, also handled the sweets at the king's table. He excelled so greatly in the latter chore that he published some seminal books on cooking and pastry-making. The most famous were *Le Cuisinier François* and *Le Pâtissier François*—François being the name by which Lavarenne referred to himself.

Lavarenne's books were best sellers among the aristocrats of Paris and the provinces. This fact reflected the growing passion, among the upper classes of Henri's reign, for haute cuisine, and for the presentation of an elegant table as a hallmark of gentility, sophistication, and refinement.

BASICS

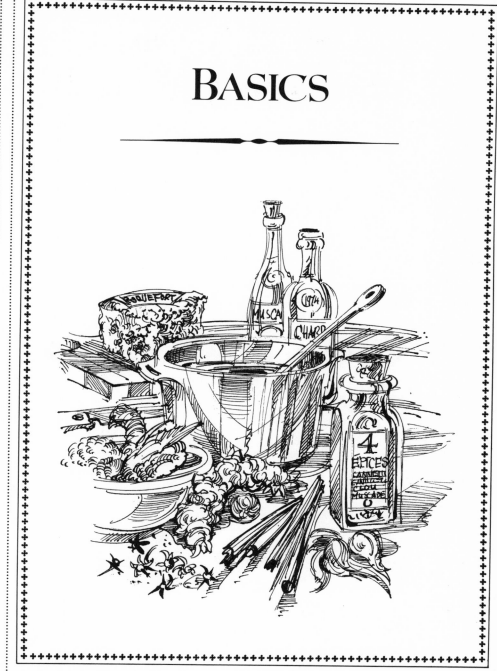

Fond de Volaille

POULTRY STOCK

If you reserve the wings, necks, and carcasses from ducks and chickens, you will be able to make a concentrated stock that will ensure flavorful sauces. Save those poultry parts in your freezer until you have 6 to 8 pounds.

6 to 8 pounds poultry parts,
chicken, duck, or a mix
4 carrots, peeled
3 leeks, trimmed and washed
3 celery stalks

3 medium turnips, peeled
4 garlic cloves, peeled
7 quarts cold water
3 onions, peeled and halved
2 cups red wine

Preheat broiler.

Place the poultry parts, carrots, leeks, celery, turnips, and garlic in a large stockpot. Cover the water and bring to a boil over high heat. Boil for $\frac{1}{2}$ hour, skimming off the fat.

Meanwhile, place the onion halves on a baking sheet, cut side up, and grill under the broiler until they are very dark, almost burnt. Add them to the pot.

Lower the heat so the stock is at a very low simmer and cook for 6 hours. Pass the stock through a fine sieve lined with a clean linen towel. At this point you will have a light stock that you can use for soups and poaching liquid. To use in sauces, it should be stronger; return the stock to the pot, add the wine, and reduce it to 1 quart over high heat. Let the stock cool and freeze it in $\frac{1}{2}$-cup containers.   [*Yield: 1 quart*]

Grilled Onions

The sauces and stocks at the Hôtel de France are famous not only for their heady flavor, but also for their hearty amber tint which adds a visual richness to the pleasure of the repast. Daguin's secret? Adding a char-grilled onion to the pot.

Cut a medium onion in half and place the halves under the broiler, cut side up. Grill the onion until it is very dark, almost burned. Add the grilled onion to the rest of the ingredients and proceed with the recipe as usual. Your soup or stock will take on a deep amber color.

Quatre Épices

FOUR SPICES

"Four spices" is a mixture of ground spices often used to flavor various dishes, especially stews and *confit*. There is no real recipe for *quatre épices*. Every cook has his or her own blend, sometimes combining more than four spices. It is basically a mixture of cinnamon, black pepper, nutmeg, and cloves. Be careful with the cinnamon. Its pungency will vary depending on its freshness, and too much can overpower the other spices.

2 tablespoons ground cloves
2 tablespoons ground nutmeg
2 tablespoons ground black
pepper

1 teaspoon cinnamon

Combine all the ingredients in an airtight container and store in a dry place. [*Yield: About $\frac{1}{3}$ cup*]

Graisse de Canard

RENDERED DUCK FAT

Rendered duck fat is essential in Gascon cooking. It gives a very distinctive flavor to many dishes. Rendered duck fat can be stored in the refrigerator for several months. After the fat is melted and removed from the pan, the leftover skins can be returned to the pot and slowly fried until they are crisp and have a deep golden color. These crispy, crackling *"fritons"* are often served with drinks or tossed in salads.

2 pounds duck skin and fat, cut into small pieces

1 cup water

Place the duck fat in a medium-size saucepan. Pour the water over it and bring to a boil. Lower the heat to a simmer and cook until the fat has melted and the water has evaporated, about 1 hour. When you hear a sizzling sound, it means the water is gone and the skin is frying. Turn off the heat and pass the fat through cheesecloth. Pour the fat into a mason jar and cool to room temperature. Refrigerate when completely cool. It will keep for up to four months.   [*Yield: 1 quart*]

Ail ou Échalotes Confits

GARLIC OR SHALLOTS CONFIT

Garlic cloves, small onions, and shallots, can be cooked *confit* style using duck or other fats. There is no need to put them in salt first, just add them to the warm fat along with the *quatre épices*. Garlic or shallot *confit* makes an excellent garnish for roasted meats or salads, and can also be used to enrich sauces.

2 garlic heads or 12 shallots
2 cups rendered duck fat (see recipe page 176)
1 teaspoon quatre épices (see recipe page 175)

$\frac{1}{4}$ teaspoon freshly ground black pepper

Peel the garlic and cut off any green sprouts within. If using shallots, cut off both ends before peeling.

Heat the duck fat in a small saucepan over medium flame. When the fat is warm, add the garlic or shallots, the *quatre épices,* and the ground pepper. Cook until they are soft, about 20 minutes for the garlic and 30 minutes for the shallots. Remove them from the fat with a slotted spoon and cool on paper towels. If they are not used immediately, they can be refrigerated in a small container for several days. Do not cover them with fat.   [*Yield: 6 servings as a garnish*]

Beurre de Roquefort

ROQUEFORT BUTTER

This is an easy recipe that comes in handy when finishing various sauces. When well wrapped, it can be kept in the refrigerator for a few weeks.

1 shallot, minced
½ cup dry white wine
10 ounces Roquefort cheese, chilled

1 cup unsalted butter (2 sticks), chilled
Salt and freshly ground black pepper to taste

Combine the minced shallot and the white wine in a small saucepan. Bring to a boil over medium heat and reduce until the liquid is almost gone. Turn off the heat and let it cool. Cut the Roquefort cheese and the butter into ½-inch cubes. Place the butter, Roquefort cheese, shallot, salt, and pepper in the bowl of a food processor. Process just until well blended. Do not overprocess or the mixture will become oily. Roll the butter into a sausage shape and wrap it in waxed paper, then plastic wrap. Refrigerate until ready to use. [*Yield: About 2 cups*]

WINES AND ARMAGNAC

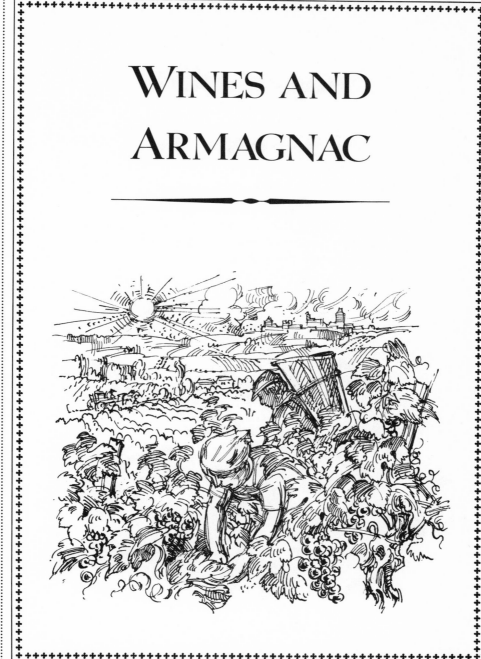

*I*t is no mere coincidence that Gascon wines have much in common with their producers. Like its people, the wines of southwest France are highly individualistic: robust and brimming with color and vigor. Certainly, the bravado of a cassoulet would outmuscle the shy, delicate wines of, say, the Loire or Alsace. These are, above all, sturdy country wines that tend to shine best on their home turf, like rugby teams. Authentic Gascon-produced wines can be difficult to find outside of the region—elsewhere in France and especially abroad. There is no huge high-tech wine-making machine operating in Gascony, but rather a discrete, low-key network of vineyards and private producers. Naturally, the local folk rather jealously reserve much of what they produce for their own thirst.

This should not, however, be a dissuasion. If you are keen to do a little detective work (and have a good relationship with your wine merchant,) you should be able to find an authentic bottle. Barring this, there are many other wines from other parts of the world which are excellent complements to the food of Gascony. The following pages describe the principal wines from the region, then discuss the best wines for particular dishes, and also suggest alternatives, should the original bottle be unobtainable in your area.

MADIRAN is a gutsy red appellation contrôlée wine, produced north of the towns of Pau and Tarbes, where the mountains subside into rolling hills freshened by the Adour. It is made primarily from a local red grape called *tannat.* Long barrel aging—twenty months or more—contributes to Madiran's rustic assertiveness. It softens considerably after six to eight years in the bottle.

CÔTES DE BUZET, also an appellation contrôlée, lies north of the Armagnac-producing region and south of the Garonne River where it slows down its tumble from the Pyrenees on its way to the Gulf of Gascony. The appellation is scattered among many communes, and it produces mostly red wine, along with some rosé and white. The reds are about 50 percent merlot and the remainder divided variously between Cabernet-Franc and Cabernet-Sauvignon. Among the best of them, Cuvée Napoléon, is comparable to a light Bordeaux. Whites are made from sémillon, sauvignon, and muscadelle grapes and are full-flavored wines with a unique undertone of smokiness.

A brace of lesser-known, but nonetheless distinguished bottles from the region are CÔTES DU MARMANDAIS and CÔTES DE DURAS. These pleasant wines

D'Artagnan

The musketeer immortalized by Alexandre Dumas was born Charles de Batz at Castelmore, circa 1620.

D'Artagnan was not the first son, and primogeniture being what it was in seventeenth-century France, second sons were forced to go out into the world to seek their fortunes. This was especially true in Gascony, where family size tended to outstrip family funds. During the sixteenth and seventeenth centuries, Gascon scions filled the armies of France.

D'Artagnan arrived in Paris in the late 1630s and joined the King's Guards, a voluntary, unpaid corps which was essentially a military training school. There he met Dumas's Porthos, Isaac de Portau from Pau. After several impressive military campaigns, he was noticed by the highly influential Cardinal Mazarin, who eventually inducted d'Artagnan into his own personal service. It was while serving as spy, soldier, and confidant to Mazarin that d'Artagnan came into contact with Louis XIV and the queen, Marie Therese. They became his friends and patrons, finally appointing him a sous-lieutenant in the musketeers in 1568.

The musketeers were a *corps d'élite* of about 150 cadets commanded by the king himself.

D'Artagnan married Charlotte de Charlecy, Dame de Saint Croix, at the Louvre in 1659 in the presence of the king and Mazarin. They had two sons, but were separated in 1665 after a history of quarrels, jealousy, and infidelity.

Undaunted by domestic unrest, d'Artagnan returned to what he did best, and was rewarded for his achievements with the rank

of Captain-lieutenant of the First Company of Musketeers, and then of General, Cavalry Brigadier. Although Dumas embellished some details for the sake of romance, unquestionably d'Artagnan led a wildly adventurous life to the last. In June of 1673, after the battle of Maastricht in the Netherlands, he was discovered dead on the field, a musketball in his throat.

are produced in the extreme north of the Gascon region, across the Garonne from the province of the Buzets, as the hills of the Massif Central interconnect with the Pyrenean hills at the fertile chevron.

Cahors, while technically from Périgord, just to the northeast of Gascony, is a heady dark red that, more than any other wine, is touted as a mate for a pot steaming with the scent of *confit* of duck, sausage, and garlic. Years ago it was known as an inky and intense wine that required a foil as muscular as cassoulet; in recent years, however, it has been tamed considerably and vinified more in the Bordeaux style. It benefits from 4 to 6 years of bottle aging.

Although *Jurançon* is made in relatively small quantities in the higher country of the Pyrenees, and therefore consumed mostly locally, it is such a regional standard that it bears mentioning. Jurançon comes in two styles: *sec* and *moelleux.* The latter is a sweet and spicy white wine often paired with a terrine of foie gras. While it does not have the finesse of a Sauternes, it has its avid followers.

WINES AND GASCON FOOD

The Holy Trinity of Gascon cuisine—foie gras, *confit de canard* (or goose), and cassoulet—are, to be sure, highly distinctive dishes, each with its own strong affinities for wine. A savory foie gras or a rich *confit* is most successfully paired with a spirited, young, acidic wine that can cut through the fat. Cassoulet, that rustic potpourri of beans, *confit,* pork, and garlic sausage, is a full-flavored and heavy dish that calls for a muscular red that can hold its own in such company.

Following is a listing of Gascon dishes and the most propitious choices from local, extraregional French and foreign wines for each.

FOIE GRAS—Of course, the method of preparation has a lot to do with the appropriate wine. A terrine of foie gras traditionally goes with good sparkling wine, either Champagne or other *méthode champenoise* wines, meaning those that have been fermented in the bottle "in the Champagne method." Scores of good sparklers from France, Spain, and the United States are widely available at moderate prices.

The other made-in-heaven match for terrine of foie gras is a quality sweet wine, such as a Sauternes, Barsac, late harvest Gewürztraminer, late harvest Riesling, and German sweet wines (in ascending order of sweetness, spätlese, auslese, beerenauslese and trockenbeerenauslese). Sweet wines are often served with foie gras as an appetizer course.

When fresh foie gras is sautéed, poached, or steamed, and accompanied by a sauce, it is often the sauce that determines the appropriate wine. As a rule of thumb, the more assertive the sauce, the more assertive the wine. At the tame end of the scale, say, sautéed foie gras with olive purée, young lively reds are lovely matches. They can be anything from the better Beaujolais to Côtes-du-Rhône, Côtes du Ventoux, so-called "petits Bordeaux," light California Cabernet Sauvignons, Merlots and gamays.

More assertive sauces, such as those with wild mushrooms, would call for bigger reds, but still those containing adequate acidity to counter the rich foie gras: young Bordeaux, heavier Côtes-du-Rhône (such as Châteauneuf-du-Pape or Hermitage), bigger California Cabernet Sauvignons and Zinfandels, Spanish Riojas, or Italian Barbarescos, to name a few.

CONFIT: When a *confit* is served crisp-skinned and supple with the traditional sautéed potatoes on the side, a bright fresh red wine brings out the best in it. Once again, a good Beaujolais or young Bordeaux with palpable tannin and acid, fit the bill. There are also scores of little-known country wines that do not rate official appellations under the French system, but which have the gutsiness to tackle the pungent herbs and meats. Similar young reds can be found in California.

CASSOULET: As noted, Cahors is a perfect match. If you can't locate a bottle of Cahors for authenticity's sake, there is no shortage of big, brawny reds in France, Spain, Italy, and the United States to marry well with this earthy stew. Any full-bodied Bordeaux with sufficient tannin would be fine as would Zinfandels and cabernets from California or Spanish wines from the Rioja region.

Armagnac, like Cognac, its counterpart from north of Bordeaux, is a brandy—that is, a distilled drink made from grapes. To fanciers of either, however, the similarities end there. Each has its distinctive style of distillation, aging, and blending. If a general image could be made, Cognac is the natty patrician who retires to the den after a formal dinner to discuss politics by the hearth, whereas Armagnac is a lusty, down-to-earth fellow who favors genial bistros and enjoys swapping tall tales with good friends. While Armagnac and Cognac do have a few qualities in common, Gascons are quick to elucidate their differences.

The region of Armagnac is in the heart of Gascony, covering three *departements:* Gers, Lot-et-Garonne and Landes. The most prestigious products come from the western region known as the *Bas-*Armagnac; it is sometimes referred to as Armagnac *Noir* because of the dense, dark forests that cover its flat, sandy terrain. Armagnac, from this subregion, is extraordinarily elegant.

The differences between Armagnac and Cognac are also climactic. Armagnac is made some eighty miles south of Cognac. The region is considerably warmer than Cognac, with salty air and sandy soil. Armagnac has been produced in Gascony, since the fourteenth century, in a special manner involving a still that resembles a lunatic double boiler—comprised of five to eight pots of copper, kept buffed and burnished to a warm ruddy glow by the assiduous attentions of the distiller. The individuals who distill Armagnac in Gascony have always been held in high regard.

From the earliest days, until the beginning of this century, the distiller would travel the roads of Gascony, from farm to farm, carrying his portable *alambic Armagnacais.* He spent several days at each farm working around the clock—once the distillation begins it cannot be halted until all is finished—turning recently harvested grapes to the coveted clear liquid that, when aged, metamorphoses into Armagnac. Today the process remains the same, although farmers bring their harvest to the farm commune, instead, to be distilled. Armagnac is distilled primarily from three grapes that thrive in the sandy regional soil—the St.-Emilion, Colombard, and Folle Blanche. The juice from those grapes is distilled to a relatively low strength—a little over 50 percent as opposed to 70 percent for Cognac. This technique infuses the Armagnac with extra flavor. The clear liquid is then aged in giant casks of black oak from the forest of Monlezun. This dark and sappy local wood gives Armagnac its unique flavor and body, and its aggressive yet smooth character.

An Armagnac aged for eight years is considered ready to drink; twelve years is even better, according to many connoiseurs. A young Armagnac is

Pousse Rapière

This Gascon cocktail is an orange-flavored liqueur of Armagnac, combined with a local sparkling wine called *vin sauvage*. It is a delicious aperitif to be enjoyed chilled.

Recipe for the *pousse rapière:* Combine one part of chilled orange-flavored Armagnac liqueur with five parts of chilled sparkling wine. Garnish with a half slice of orange.

The liquor and the sparkling wine can be ordered through liquor stores.

as feisty and bold as an adolescent; with age, however, Armagnac, like teenagers, loses its hard edge and becomes more mellow.

Armagnac bottles are marked according to the Armagnac's origin and age. Some carry the appellation Bas-Armagnac, Haut-Armagnac, or Ténaréze when they come exclusively from one of those three regions. The appellation Armagnac alone could be a blend of brandies from different regions.

The descriptions V.O., V.S.O.P., and Réserve indicate that the Armagnac has been aged at least four years in casks. The appellations Extra, Napoleon, and Vieille Réserve must have five years of wood aging. The vintage represents the year in which the grapes were harvested.

There are no monolithic companies that dominate the Armagnac trade, as with Cognac, but rather it tends to be a business of small producers.

Until a few years ago, vintage Armagnac was not available in this country. Now, one can find older Armagnac by reputable producers.

Shopping Sources

GAME: All the game mentioned in this book is easily available in good butcher shops. A few, such as quail and squab, can be purchased in some supermarkets. Depending on the season, the shops will carry frozen game; ask before buying it. Fresh game is available at d'Artagnan, Inc., 399-419 St. Paul Avenue, Jersey City, NJ 07306. Tel: 1-800-DARTAGNAN.

DUCK CONFIT, CONFIT GIZZARDS, CURED, FRESH AND SMOKED MAGRET, FRESH FOIE GRAS, FOIE GRAS TERRINE, FRESH MOULARD DUCKS, RENDERED DUCK FAT, DUCK STOCK: available by mail order at d'Artagnan, Inc. 399-419 St. Paul Avenue, Jersey City, NJ 07306. Tel: 1-800-DARTAGNAN.

Index

ABOUT THE AUTHORS

ANDRÉ DAGUIN is one of the leading Gascon chefs. Over the years he has been praised by many cooking experts for his imaginative cuisine and his outspoken views on the subject. He owns a two-star restaurant, the Hôtel de France, in Auch.

André was born in Auch, Gers, in 1935 into a family of chefs and cooks. His father was the chef and owner of the Hôtel de France since 1926, and his grandfather cooked there in 1884.

After studying at the Hotel School of Paris and working in several restaurants in the capital, André returned to Auch in 1960. He took over the family business and immediately earned his first star from the *Guide Michelin*. Over the years he developed a very personal interpretation of Gascon cooking and became the culinary ambassador of this region of France. He earned his second star in 1970. He is also the author of *Le Nouveau Cuisinier Gascon*, published in France in 1984.

André, with the help of his wife, Joceline, has made the Hôtel de France a must on the culinary maps of France.

The Daguins have three children, all pursuing careers in the gastronomic field. One of their daughters, Ariane, moved to the United States and is currently the co-owner of d'Artagnan, Inc. which distributes foie gras and game.

ANNE DE RAVEL was born in France in 1957 in Mont de Marsan, Landes. She came to the United States ten years ago.

She was food columnist for the *Hartford Courant* while she lived in Connecticut. Four years ago, she moved to New York City, where she became a freelance food consultant, working as recipe editor on various cookbooks from leading authors such as Julie Sahni and Flo Braker. She is also a food and wine consultant of *The New York Times Magazine, Entertaining Part II*. This is her first cookbook.